In Sickness
and In Health

Forthcoming Title

After Math: Life Without Sue

In Sickness and In Health

A Memoir of Love

J. S. Russo

Legwork Team Publishing
New York

Legwork Team Publishing
80 Davids Drive, Suite One
Hauppauge, NY 11788
www.legworkteam.com
Phone: 631-944-6511

Legwork Team
Publishing

This book is a work of non-fiction. Unless otherwise noted, the author and the publisher make no explicit guarantees as to the accuracy of the information contained in this book and in some cases; names of people and places have been altered to protect their privacy.

First edition 8/19/2009

Printed in the United States of America
This book is printed on acid-free paper

TESTIMONIALS

"I found, In Sickness and In Health *to be an amazing story, well written and extremely moving. I've been 'there' and can relate to your experiences. Your book is powerful and will no doubt inspire others to fight through this horrible disease."*
—Steve Cohen, EVP & COO
St. Martin's Press Trade Publishing Group

"This memoir exhibits the unconditional love between a couple with a passion for life, as they travel down that 'long and winding road.' It will really make you believe that 'it is better to have loved and lost than never to have loved at all.'"
—Cathy Kimura RN, Oncology Nurse

"To share their journey through Joe's beautiful and sensitive writings is very special! He not only reflects on the medical aspects, but also on the incredible relationship they shared together as husband and wife, and best friends. Throughout their journey, they continued to give each other the strength, at times the tenderness and humor to meet each challenge. Joe, may all my patients have the unselfish support, devotion, and love that Susan had from you."
—Dr. Virginia E. Maurer, Diseases and Surgery of the Breast

"In Sickness and In Health: A Memoir of Love" is a tender love story about one couple's journey through the maze of breast cancer and the war they declared against it. It is at times humorous and uplifting with accounts of zany, madcap events, juxtaposed against the frightening diagnosis, treatments and the recurrence of cancer, and how through it all, their undying love for each other prevailed and even flourished. It is a story of Sue and Joe, two courageous, intelligent, and loveable people trying to live a normal family life filled with hope and joy, despite the heart wrenching diagnosis and the inescapable end that would surely come."

—Jane G. Howard RN, Oncology Nurse

"Your story is beautiful and heart wrenching. The love that you shared with Sue was an incredible thing to read about-it seemed to me to be the kind of love that everyone dreams of having. You have an incredible voice and power in your words. At times, your prose grabbed my heart and would not let go, while other times you made me laugh out loud."

—Katrina Hill, Editor

"This is a rich and warm account of the strength of a marriage. It is a tale of how our limits are tested and the resilience a family must find while watching a loved one endure the hardships of cancer. It reminds us that health is a gift one must never take for granted."

—Dr. Bret Ostrager, South Shore Family Medicine

"How very fortunate that Joe and Sue had one another. The love they shared with each other and their children is what every young girl dreams about. Her prince will come and they will be happy ever after. Their story though tragic at the end was really quite beautiful. Their love filled the room and made everyone smile. While so many of us who have cancer understand the anguish and pain, knowing that you have someone who cares and walks that path alongside you somehow makes it easier. Sue left a legacy of great spirit and a will to live. She shared with all of us through Joe that while her life was cut short she made the best of every second. Those memories will be cherished for all time. I am proud to have known Sue and the wonderful family she leaves behind. This book instills in all of us how precious life is and how important the time is that we are here on this earth. Joe will always think about Sue with that incredible smile and warmth."

—Geri Barish, Survivor
President 1 in 9 Breast Cancer Organization
Executive Director Hewlett House

This book is dedicated to the life of Susan—
my soul mate, my best friend, my lover, my wife—
and to our two incredibly wonderful, compassionate,
good-hearted children, Matthew and Justin.
It is also dedicated to all those who have endured the
hardships of cancer, either passed on or with us today.
We do feel the pain that you feel, but also sense your
hopefulness of a brighter tomorrow.

"Loved By All She Touched"

"Dancing With The Angels"

CONTENTS

Foreword . . . . *xv*

Preface . . . . *xix*

Acknowledgments . . . .*xxiii*

The Beginning 1

Connections and Destiny 11

Bicycle Boardwalk 19

Grandma Interruptus 27

Our Wedding 35

Our Early Married Life Together 41

Pyramid Visit 47

"Typhoid" Susan 57

The Birth of Our Children 63

Shandi 69

Nine Months of Chemotherapy 83

Music in Our Lives 95

Sounds and Sense Memories 105

CONTENTS

50 and in the Pink 121

The Port 127

The Amazons. 133

Idiosyncrasies, OCD, Mystic Powers, and Superstitions. . 149

Numerology and Letters 163

The Five-year Myth. 167

9-11 Morning 187

The Oprah Letter. 195

Our Healing Movies. 201

God Forbid. 209

Be Aware of Flying Objects or Hammer Time 213

Introducing Spinal Tap—It Rocked Our World 229

The New Millennium 235

The Final Page in the Photo Album 241

About the Author. *267*

Susan Satriano Foundation. *269*

FOREWORD
By Robert Anthony

Finding a soul mate is hard. Losing a soul mate is much harder. That was the unfortunate situation my brother, Joe Russo, had to face when the love of his life, Susan, was diagnosed with breast cancer. After sixteen years of marriage to the woman who was unquestioningly his perfect match, he was forced to face the prospect of life without Sue. As you would expect, that diagnosis literally changed the time and tenor of their lives.

This book tells the story of how Joe, Sue, and their two boys, Matthew and Justin, lived, loved, and lost their thirteen-year battle with cancer. Along the way, they learned much about the illness, the doctors, the medications, and about each other. And I learned about my brother—about his true character, his deep love for Sue, and his inner strength.

Joe's inner strength was an attribute I had not previously seen. After all, he was my *little* brother, the kid who always followed my lead, who was unschooled in the ways of the world, and who never even dated until he was in college.

Joe was the little boy who let the waves of life thrust him along; the quiet little puppy who followed happily behind his friends, and the good little boy who followed all of his parents' wishes, rules, and regulations without question.

Was this a person who could face adversity head-on and deal with the harsh realities that life had dealt him and his family? I didn't think so, but I was very wrong.

Beginning with Sue's cancer diagnosis, my brother grew into a man who did everything in his power to help his wife live a better and longer life. He did not retreat into a shell, leaving Sue alone to deal with her thoughts of mortality; instead he left his job to support her at home in every way possible. He did not simply accept without question what the medical professionals told him were certainties about treatments and outcomes; instead, he learned all he could about those treatments and outcomes and became Sue's best advocate with their countless doctors, nurses, and technicians.

Outwardly, Joe became the pillar of strength to his family, friends, and to me. I simply did not understand how he could appear to handle their hardships, setbacks, and pending loss so well. I know now that it was because of his desire to be strong for his soul mate, Sue—to help her in every way he could during her time of need and to simply be there for her. Joe was no faint individual, as I had perceived him to be when we grew up; instead, he was now a man filled with strength of character and deep love for his wife.

So, when Joe told me he wanted to write a book about their experiences, I should have known he was up to the task. My first thought, however, was that he was a *math* teacher, not an author—excellent at *square* roots, but not that great at *word* roots. Could he write a book about such a deeply personal experience so that readers would get a true insight into what it was like to live with cancer for thirteen years? The answer is a resounding, "Yes."

As he relates his life with Sue, Joe will reach out to you and pull you into their world. You will laugh, cry, and learn about living and loving with the cloud of cancer constantly overhead. But you will also discover that this period need not reduce itself to a mere countdown to death, a time of passivity in which you meekly accept the inevitable. This time can, and should, also be a time to value your friends, family, and loved ones—a time to *do*, to fight, to be together, and to live your life.

In the end, my "little" brother stood tall and showed his inner strength: he left his job to be with and support Sue during every minute of her disease; he did the right things *for* her and the good things *with* her. He did the things that a good soul does for his true soul mate. As a result, he knew, his children knew, and Sue knew that we are here to love each other—in good times, in bad times, in sickness and in health.

Robert Anthony,
brother of J. S. Russo

PREFACE

Writing *In Sickness and In Health: A Memoir of Love* was a cathartic labor of love. I really can't even call it a labor because it wasn't. It actually became a leisurely pastime of mine that allowed my emotions to spew forth. It was self-therapy; a "lie down on the couch and let's talk about it" session I was conducting with myself. It was written with multiple purposes in mind.

I started a charity in Sue's honor back in 2006, the Susan Satriano Memorial Scholarship Foundation. We no longer teach, yet there was a burning desire to continue to help children. I can still "teach" through the Foundation's scholarship awards. I am happy to say that net proceeds from the sales of *In Sickness and In Health: A Memoir of Love* will go directly to the Foundation to keep it alive and well enabling it to continue to assist students in the future.

Another purpose for writing the book was that it certainly conjured up many great memories for me; some sad, some joyful, but one thing for sure, emanating from every page was the love between two people through the good and bad times. I wrote each paragraph as if you and I were having a conversation in my living room, reminiscing about the life that Sue and I shared together—two everyday people who seemed destined to meet, fall in love, and enjoy great times together, but also to endure difficult periods as well.

Thirdly, as you read through the book, remember that even though Sue and I were dealt a bad hand, we still managed to play and stay in the game at a very high level, sometimes needing to bluff ourselves into dreaming of a happy existence, while other times not requiring a facade because times were actually joyous and peaceful. My hope is that this book will inspire you to move forward, no matter how bad things become. It conveys this very powerful message: we are all struck by hurtful moments or extended periods of suffering in our lives, some severe, some just a bruising, but it's how we deal with the hurt and pain that makes us, us. Sue and I faced cancer head on and squarely everyday, yet carried on doing good things for others and ourselves while living a fruitful and joyous life. I understand that Sue's situation was conducive to this—she was young when she was diagnosed and her body was strong enough to take chemotherapy, then rebound back to "normalcy" to continue on with life. I do realize that this may not be the case for others, but please remember that cancer does not have to be a death sentence. Try not to waste time figuring out what might be in your future, but instead enjoy what is now. To those of you who are cancer patients, and those of you who are caregivers, trust me when I say this is easier said than done. But it is essential to your own well-being and sanity if you can pull it off. Sue and I struggled with this very concept, but to our credit for the majority of the time, we didn't let cancer stop us; we lived, we enjoyed, and we loved what we had in our world.

Ultimately, I hope this book will demonstrate that you can have fun even though cancer, the underlying theme, is dreadful. If you are going through this disease or know someone who is battling it presently, I want you to laugh and be amused, roll in the aisles, and let your hair down at times because Lord knows, the cancer will supply you with enough sadness and tears. Some of the events I wrote about in the book that occurred in our lives were hilarious whether Sue was inflicted with cancer or not. Not only is laughter good for healing and good for your soul, it allows you the time to escape from the ravages of cancer for maybe a moment, and if you're lucky, maybe longer. Sue and I did our very best to live by this credo; after all you get only one shot here…make it a great time!

ACKNOWLEDGMENTS

A great debt of gratitude goes to all of the professionals that Sue and I met along our long and eventful journey, including the doctors, the nurses, and the office staffers. And what can you say about family and friends? They supported us with their presence and thoughtful, meaningful sentiments all the time. They were there with Sue and me to share every laugh and every tear. To our incredible children, Matthew and Justin, we thank you for who you are and what you have become and appreciate all that you both had to endure. We know that you are gentler, kinder, and stronger because of the experience.

Transforming this memoir of love into the book you now hold, could only become a reality through the dedicated efforts of Yvonne Kamerling and Janet Yudewitz of Legwork Team Publishing. I'm especially appreciative of their continued patience and guidance.

Legwork Team Publishing utilizes a number of skilled professionals to obtain quality results. I want to acknowledge Gayle Newman for her artistic design, layout and art direction. I also want to thank Katrina Hill and Russell Sacco for sensitively reviewing my original manuscript and infusing their invaluable editorial insights throughout the production process.

I wish to gratefully acknowledge the following music rights administrators for granting permission to use song lyrics in this memoir that were especially meaningful to Sue and me:

The Beginning

Ｓeptember 2, 1992. That date mean anything to you? Probably not. We Americans were ending the Bush Senior years and preparing for the onset of the Clinton years. As for me, Joe Russo, I was preparing for another school year at Parkland High School. I had taught Mathematics there since 1977 and loved the school, the kids, and of course, my colleagues.

It was the first day of the new school year, so the faculty gathered in the High School cafeteria at 7:30 in the morning to shoot the breeze with our teacher friends that we hadn't seen or had much contact with over the two-month summer vacation. A beautiful spread of bagels, danishes, fruit, juice, and coffee was in place to welcome us back. Parkland certainly knew how to do it up! I was not too hungry or talkative that day— something highly unusual for me. I was a pretty popular guy at school, always ready with a pun or joke to lighten the mood if needed. I was the one who appeared before the school board and asked, with a straight face, if in March when clocks were shifted forward, could it be done during my third period class? I was the one that produced a funny yet poignant retirement video for a dear colleague of ours from the department. The Math department always turned to me to supply the frivolity. But that day was different. My colleagues noticed it too. Many came by to ask me if I was okay. They could see that I wasn't very attentive or interested in their summer exploits.

At 8:15 a.m., or thereabout, we were herded like cattle into the auditorium to hear the speech of our new Superintendent. Most people anxiously waited to "size" the new man up, hoping that he would be a "human being" and not one of those "ivory tower" educators that took off for the greener pastures of "administrationville." Me…I was like the dog that's being spoken to by his owner in a Gary Larsen *Far Side* cartoon. All I heard was blah, blah, blah, blah, Parkland…blah, blah, blah, Parkland. While the goals for the district that coming academic year were being spouted forth, left and right, from the new Superintendent, my mind was miles away!

You see, back home was my best friend, lover, confidant, my world, and my wife of sixteen wonderful years, Sue, waiting for probably the most important, potentially life altering phone call of our lives. Sue had been experiencing pain in the upper quadrant of her left breast for much of the summer. She saw some doctors about it, only to be told that there is no apparent problem. She had what I would call the "high price feel-up" on her breast by specialists on numerous occasions that summer. She just knew that something was not right. She took mammograms to expose any potential problems. The technicians told her that if she wasn't feeling pain, it couldn't be cancer. Sue noticed that the technicians were never really focusing their state-of-the-art scanners on the upper quadrant where she was feeling the discomfort. Sue also made it very clear to all of the professionals that she had lost her Mother to breast cancer back in 1983. With all these factors in place, Sue insisted that a needle biopsy be done to extricate some of her breast tissue. These were the results we were waiting to hear on September 2, 1992.

I don't know how I made it through that day at school, and Lord knows how Sue did it as well at home. The one thing that Sue and I were never good at was what to do while waiting for medical results to arrive. It was almost like we played a brutal game with each other to see who would crack first, who would say the first word, who would declare the obvious fear, who would cry first. Inevitably, it was me, though we often would not say anything for fear of jinxing the result. Sometimes we would stare at each other for what seemed to be hours on end, not uttering a word—just staring. The silence was deafening. Other times we would talk out every possible scenario, the good and the bad. I guess this way, whatever was told to us had already been "strategized" out by us; no one could tell us anything that we haven't already prepared for. Another technique that we used was to think the result was going to be the worst. That way, if that was truly what the result was, we were prepared for it. If it was a good result, we would be pleasantly surprised and elated when it came. I think of all of the time Sue and I wasted worrying about what was out of our hands anyway. What it was, it was! We could have been living life during those periods of time rather than dreading it. If I could only have those wasted hours back…sigh!

I broke all Indianapolis 500 speed records to get home that day from school in the afternoon. I had a tremendous headache all day long. The gears in my head were grinding, churning, thinking, thinking, and thinking. I knew no call from the doctor was received because I was in constant contact with Sue all day long by phone. When I arrived at home, it was time to employ one of our "coping" strategies. That day, we used the "discuss all the possibilities" method. I guess we needed to talk to each other because we were both terrified inside.

Around four in the afternoon, the phone rang. It was a piercing ring that cut through our eardrums and our hearts. Sue remained where she was on the couch in the living room while I ran to answer it. I picked up the phone, and it was the doctor with the results of the biopsy. The words that I remember him saying were "atypical cells." I asked what that meant. Mind you, this was the doctor who had told us all summer long that everything was fine. It was no surprise to me that in his attempt to describe atypical cells to me, the word cancer was never mentioned. Instead, I heard a number of possibilities as to why the cells might be atypical. He said that the cells might have been pressed too tightly on the microscope slide causing them to be misshapen. He said that there might have been too much dye on the slide. He probably went on to say a number of other reasons for this to happen, but by now, I was once again the dog in the Larsen cartoon. Sue and I were not quite sure what to do with this information. We obviously did not like the idea of atypical anything! This is not what we were hoping for. We hugged and cried on the couch for a good long time. We needed to get that out of our system before we could sensibly plan our next move.

As much as we wanted to believe the doctor, we couldn't help thinking about all of the factors that proved him wrong: the cancer in Sue's family history; the fact that we lived on Long Island where in the early 1900s potato farmers would use all kinds of pesticides and fertilizers that seeped into water supplies; power lines were all above ground emitting electric waves into the environment; we ate foods with high fat content; and the fact that our neighborhood block had a number of cancer cases. I could go on and on, which is exactly what was going on in our minds—swirling thoughts of possibilities, a non-stop merry-go-round of thoughts and feelings, except these thoughts were far from merry. At times like this, we both should have been heavy drinkers. Nothing would have bothered us at all. Instead, we'd probably feel pretty good about things. Unfortunately, hot cocoa made my head spin, so heavy imbibing was not the solution!

We did a lot of soul searching that evening. We went through an anger stage asking why did this happen to us. Then we would say to each other that, at this point in time, we really didn't know if ANYTHING had happened. We didn't know if the doctor's non-cancer diagnosis was correct or not. It was this constant bombardment of contradictions that drove us crazy. Probably due to mental exhaustion, Sue and I fell asleep in each other's arms on the couch that evening. How fitting...neither of us letting go, reaching out for each other's strength to get through this nerve-racking problem.

The next morning, I called Parkland to explain what we had found out the previous day, and I didn't go in to work because of it. Sue and I had discussed that we couldn't leave the situation as it was without pursuing it further. We were quickly learning that you must be your own advocate. You know your body better than any professional, and it was becoming clear that we needed to take the initiative. Chancing that this could potentially be cancer, time was of the essence, especially remembering that Sue was experiencing these awkward, uncomfortable feelings since early that summer.

We decided that we needed to get in touch with the doctor to have more tissue removed and biopsied. We scheduled this procedure to be done the next day. Once again, we felt that we were back to square one. All of the possibilities of yesterday still remained unsolved and unanswered.

Sue and I tried to divert attention from tomorrow's procedure by doing crossword puzzles. Sue, though a math major, had a great vocabulary and could do any word related game as well as anyone. She would always solve the *Wheel of Fortune* puzzles well before the contestants. She would get the answers even before Vanna could move her vowels!

❧❧❧

That reminds me of a funny thing Sue once did to my dad. Dad also, was very good at word games, but truly, not in Sue's class. One night Sue and I were over at my parents' home. We discovered that _Wheel of Fortune_ aired on channel 10 thirty minutes before it did on channel 7. My dad wasn't aware of this little fact. So Sue and I watched the earlier version, and remembered all of the answers. Sue then challenged my dad to solve the puzzles on the later showing before she did. Now dad was always up for a challenge, so he agreed, and they both sat in front of the television watching very intently. Truly, Sue didn't need this extra help, but it turned out to be hilarious when Sue got the first puzzle after only two letters showing. Dad was very impressed. She went on to do this a couple more times, at which point dad knew something was up. After ten minutes, we stopped laughing, and we admitted that Sue had just a little extra help. It was all in good-natured fun.

❧❧❧

On this particular day, though, Sue wasn't getting many crossword puzzles correct. Neither was I. Knowing the name of the capital of Tibet was as far from our thoughts as Tibet itself. We tried listening to music. We took a walk around the neighborhood, all the while fearing what terrible news we might find out tomorrow. We talked about the scenarios extensively. We tried to eat something for dinner, but nothing tasted right. Our stomachs were rumbling with nervous anticipation; another day of worry, sadness, and despair. We had an early bedtime due to the fact that we needed to be at the hospital at 7:30 in the morning.

We got up at 5 a.m., showered, got dressed, and drove to the hospital. We felt like we were a funeral procession of only one car going to find out a deadly diagnosis. When we arrived, the hospital attendants were very pleasant. They took Sue away to prep her. I made sure that I would see her again before the procedure was started. They assured me that they would wheel her out for me to say what I needed to say. All the while Sue was away, I thought of the right things to say to her; encouragement, hope, support, and especially, no matter what happened, how I much I loved her. I got the opportunity to see her as the hospital nurses had promised. I asked for a few minutes alone with her, and they granted my request. I tried to hold back the tears as I said what I wanted to say. Sue, outwardly, was a rock. She was steady, prepared, and actually tried to console me. But she also looked so fragile laying there on the gurney. I kissed and hugged her and wished her good luck as they wheeled her away from me. I started to cry uncontrollably.

Hours went by, though it felt like days. Finally, the doctor came out to the waiting room. I quickly stood up to acknowledge his presence in the room. I sensed that what he had to tell me was not good. He started by putting his arm around my shoulders and invited me to sit down. By that time I was terrified, and I started to shake. I will never forget his first words to me. He said that he couldn't believe it was cancer and that he was so sure it wasn't going to be. That was it—the word "cancer." Our fears had now become a reality.

CANCER…CANCER…CANCER. That is all I heard, and I started to shake and cry. All he could say at that point was that he was sorry. I was stunned, shocked, and immobile in disbelief. The doctor left the room, and I was left there with my thoughts and the reality that Sue had cancer. I thought about Sue, where she was and how I needed desperately to be with her. How she was going to deal with this news? What must she be thinking? How are we going to tell our kids, Matthew and Justin? I felt so bad for Sue and felt so helpless and lonely. I felt like Sue had just been given her death sentence. All of our hopes and dreams were shattered in one single moment; by one single word—CANCER. I needed to see Sue, and I needed to see her immediately.

A nurse came into the room, telling me how sorry she was about the news. She proceeded to tell me that due to the anesthesia, Sue was in the recovery room and had not yet been informed about the diagnosis. I told the nurse that I wanted to be the one to tell her. Another hour passed and all the while, I needed to find the right thing to say to my beloved Sue. I thought of all the encouraging things I could say: how we are going to fight this, how many advances were made in the study of cancer every day, and how I would support her to the fullest. I thought of all those things, but when they wheeled a half-dazed Sue into the room, I lost it. I collapsed over her body and blurted out screaming that it was cancer. Sue was still semi-groggy and didn't quite hear what I said. I cried it out to her again. Her eyes half glazed over, and in a soft voice Sue questioned, "It's cancer?" Before I could respond, she fell asleep again. If I could have those moments back, I would have said all the right things I had wanted to say. I blew it. My raw emotion poured out, and I knew that it really didn't do any good for Sue to hear this news in that way. I blew it and I was so sorry. I needed to be strong for her and I wasn't. I knew that I would be there for Sue. That was never the question. I loved her in health, and I would love her in sickness as well. Could I be strong for Sue? That was something I needed to prove to her…and to myself.

Connections and Destiny

Sue and I were probably destined to be together. Before we knew of each other's existence, we shared so much in common. We both skipped third grade in our respective elementary schools. In my case, I later realized that I peaked out academically in that grade—everything else was downhill from there. It's tough to know that your best academic days are already behind you after third grade.

Sue was born on July 20, 1952. That day in 1969 became the day that man took "one small step, but one giant leap for mankind." I was born April 22, 1952. That day in the 70s became the day to be aware of our planet and its beauty, Earth Day. Sue and I were the earth and moon! In honor of this, I made Sue a homemade birthday card for her 34th birthday which also was our tenth wedding anniversary year, 1986. The front of the card showed Sue's face, peering out through the visor of the spacesuit she is wearing on the moon. I didn't have the technical know-how to do this feat on the computer, so I simply printed a page with a spaceman bounding on the moon's surface and then used a scissors to cut the visor portion out and stuck a picture of Sue behind it. The words say, "One great event happened on this day in history...." When Sue opened the card, there was a beautiful headshot of her, looking so pretty, while the remainder of the caption read, "You touched down on this earth! I love you very much. Happy Birthday." Thinking about it brings tears to my eyes. Even though it was primitively produced (I only knew of one type of mouse at the time—Mickey!), Sue appreciated the attempt, but really loved the sentiment. I keep that card in a safe place, even today.

There were other ties between us as well. I was a big sports fan, following the New York Yankees and other New York teams also. Sue...well, she claimed to be a fan. I guess when you first meet and you are infatuated with each other, you want to show interest in your partner's hobbies and the like. So she kind of stretched the truth just a bit!

Seeing that she really didn't know the difference between a gridiron from a clothes iron, a baseball diamond from a jeweler's diamond, or a basketball hoop from an earring hoop, I told her that I was going to take her to a "professional" hockey game. Of course at the time, I couldn't afford a ticket to the Nassau Coliseum to see the New York Islanders play or a seat at Madison Square Garden to witness the Rangers skate, but I could spend a dollar to gain admission to Abe Stark Rink in Brooklyn to see the high school kids compete in a New York Police Athletic League. What the heck—to Sue, it was professional, right? The venue was freezing (almost like no one had paid the heating bill). We sat down on the cold, metallic, bleacher-type benches after buying a couple of hot chocolates, clutching them close to our bodies just to try to get some warmth. Sue was being a trooper, but a few minutes after the opening puck was dropped, she turned to me and asked if we had to stay for all nine innings. I spit out the hot chocolate I was presently imbibing, and after I stopped belly laughing, I looked at her and said, "Maybe we can stay just until the seventh inning stretch?"

We found over the years, that even if liking sports wasn't a common point, it didn't matter. Sue and I had a good time being together and we wanted to be together, no matter what the venue. Actually, the colder the management kept the building, the more we needed to nestle and huddle up together. Lower the temperature a couple more degrees, would you, Mr. Stark?

♥♥♥

Sue and I shared a "six degrees of separation" connection. You know, if you work your life's path back long enough, they say we all have ties somewhere down the line. Well, that was the case with Sue and me. My seventh grade math teacher in John Wiliston Junior High School years later became Sue's Math Chairman at Bushnick High School where she taught classes for ten years. How about that for validating six degrees of separation, karma, destiny, or whatever you want to call it.

We met at Brooklyn College in a math class. Sue would tell you that that was the only D grade she ever received in a college math class. As for me, I did great in the class. You see, I had no idea that I was being pursued due to my being naive about women and relationships. Sue turned out to be my true first love. (I don't count the infantile crush I had on my 7th grade earth science teacher!)

It was around Christmas 1973 that Sue invited herself to my apartment to help me decorate the tree. For Sue, this was a novelty since she was Jewish. For little old naive me, it was a nice person looking to help make my tree more festive. She brought over some beautiful ornaments, which to this day are still hung on the tree annually. At the time, I thought that she must have spent a great deal of money on the ornaments. I found out later, after we were married, that Sue had told her mom that she thought she found "the one" and her mom, bless her soul, took her shopping for some nice Christmas items. Sue's mom knew that the way to get a good Christian boy's heart was by decorating his tree with some fine looking Christmas ornaments. Boy, she knew what she was talking about!

Then there was the first time that I ventured to Sue's place. She lived with her parents in Brighton Beach in Brooklyn. Now Brighton is a world unto itself! There is the famous boardwalk and beach, the main drag named Brighton Beach Avenue with its elevated train and assorted internationally flavored shops. The people of Brighton, as I found out, felt that as long as the elevated train stood, they were protected. It didn't matter that the light was red for them and green for me, they still had the right of passage because nothing could possibly happen to them—they were protected by being under the "El" (elevated train). By the way, this is still true to this day! The El, with its trains clicking and clacking on the old rusty tracks overhead, and the sparks from its third rail flaming down onto Brighton Beach Avenue did and still does have a magical power. I, too, have used its mystic power to avoid onrushing cars and buses—there is something to it!

Anyway, back to my first visit to Sue's apartment. I needed directions to get there so Sue graciously supplied them to me over the phone. I should have seen what I was in for when she told me to make a left turn when I see an establishment named "The Store on 6th Street" which just happened to be located on Brighton 4th Street. True, there was a store on that corner, and that was its name. Despite the strange location of that schlock-ridden corner store, I made it to the apartment. I knocked on the door and Sue's dad greeted me for the very first time. We shook hands and he led me into the living room. I found out years later after Sue and I were married that her dad told her I had a very flaccid handshake. Apparently putting my virility in question was not a great way to start a relationship with his daughter. We always had a good chuckle over that in the years to come. I made sure to give him the Incredible Hulk rock solid handshake from that moment on. Sue was sitting on the couch awaiting my arrival. The living room furniture was situated with the back of the couch abutting a floor to ceiling mirror. Sue and I sat on that couch and began to talk when her little sister Terri came into the room. Terri at the time was maybe 11 years old and was very, very curious about her sister's newly found friend. She hung around us and when Sue and I gave her little to no attention, Terri started to dance in front of us, keeping one eye on the mirror to make sure her dance steps looked good, and one eye on us wondering when we were going to acknowledge her presence in the room. It was all very cute for a while but Sue and I really wanted to be anywhere we could be alone. If my memory serves me, I believe the man who thought my handshake was Jell-O came to our rescue and took Terri out for a walk on the boardwalk. Finally Sue and I were together by ourselves. I was a bit nervous and I didn't budge off that seat the entire visit. Sue could see that I was a novice at this dating thing, but she was great. It was so easy and comfortable to be with her because she made you feel that way. It was as if I'd known her all my life. She had that ability to make you feel right at home. That helped to loosen me up and we ended up having had lots to say to each other. We sat on that living room couch for hours just talking about our experiences at college, our respective families and friends, and life in general. It was great. My first real experience with a girl was so positive; we did this quite often during the weeks to come.

I would be remiss if I didn't tell you that I did do some

pre-investigative work to find out exactly who Sue was. While she was attending Brooklyn College, Sue was waitressing part time at this dumpy looking restaurant in Brooklyn called The Flame. Sue would be the first to tell you that this was not going to be her lifelong profession. The way she did her job, I was amazed it was her daylong profession. She never quite mastered the art of holding many trays at once, but she did very well at mopping up and cleaning after the trays hit the tile-laden floors. You know what, I didn't mind a bit. You see, as I was peering through the windows of the restaurant from the outside, and saw Sue in her little waitress uniform bending over to clean up the mess, the view was fantastic. Sue was, as the kids say now, eye candy—from any angle or position.

One of the classes you must take when you are preparing to become a teacher is something called Student Teaching. What this entailed was a five-day a week commitment to observe a veteran teacher in the classroom while you take notes and learn what to do, and sometimes, what not to do. Occasionally, the veteran teacher would throw you a bone and have you teach one his classes while he did the observing. I invited myself the day that Sue was to teach a lesson; part of my pre-investigative work once again. Sue had the class of misfit kids to teach that day. She had these kids enthralled with her lesson on signed numbers. Maybe it was the blue and orange miniskirt, or should I call it an extended belt, and the formfitting Danskin top. She sat cross-legged on the front desk spouting out rules and theorems about math, but no one seemed to mind, not even the "convict-like" kids she was addressing. I told her afterwards that she and Betty Grable have a lot in common. Sue had it all—looks, brains, body, a good sense of humor. Who could ask for anything more? My mission was accomplished, and I thought that for my first ever girlfriend, I couldn't do better than Sue. You know, I was right!

Bicycle Boardwalk

y 1973, Sue and I were dating full force. The set-up couldn't have been any better. I lived with a roommate in Bensonhurst, Brooklyn, and Sue was living at home with her parents and sisters in Brighton Beach, Brooklyn. These two areas of Brooklyn were two exits away if you drove on the Belt Parkway, a roadway that loops around Brooklyn and parts of Queens. Finding a spot to put the car was, and always will be a real difficult task near Sue, though. With alternate side parking and limited curb space, it was always better to ride my bike to her house. Connecting her part of town with mine was a wide, spacious, wooden-planked boardwalk that paralleled the beach and Atlantic Ocean. Its expanse included communities from Coney Island to Manhattan Beach. On a nice day, it was a pleasure to get a little pedaling exercise as well as enjoy the idyllic scene of the waves ebbing and flowing on the golden sand.

I should point out that this apartment in Bensonhurst literally fell into my lap. At the time, my brother was getting married and his ex-roommate needed a replacement for Bob. I knew this fellow from our days back in the Canarsie projects where we all grew up. I would be the little brother "cling-on" tagging along sometimes with the older group, namely Bob and his friend. But I was no longer a secondary thought because I was needed to fill the void in the shared apartment.

My parents were moving out to Shirley, Long Island simultaneously with Bob's impending nuptials. Now, Shirley was a ghost town, just starting to be developed with homes, businesses, and schools back at that time. The Sunrise Highway, presently a bustling, vibrant route to get out east, was just a future thought in some town planner's mind in Suffolk County.

At the time, my mother, coming from the "old" country in Italy, was not exactly doing cartwheels over my dating a Jewish girl. Dad really let things be, but he was placed right smack in the middle of a maelstrom. What probably also bothered mom more than anything else was that I was not religious. Heck, I disliked attending church services and receiving religious instructions as a kid, never quite understanding why I was there and what I could gain by going. So she did all she could to entice me out to "God's Country," excuse the expression! She even spoke to the Superintendant of schools in Shirley to see if there might be a teaching position for her presently unemployed son. I found out much later that she did secure a math position at Shirley High School and mom had a room painted my favorite color in the house they were presently building. This room, for 1973, had all the amenities a twenty-one year old boy would want: stereo/hi-fi, color television, a very comfortable bed, and even a Lava Lamp! It became affectionately known as the "Blue Room"...almost "White House" sounding!

One problem with her scheme: Sue was in Brooklyn and I'd be in Shirley. The distance might as well have been from here to eternity. Our relationship would have been doomed to failure...score one for mom! The other issue was that even though New York City had put a freeze on Math Teacher's Licensing Exams due to budgetary difficulties the city was encountering, my Brooklyn College professor had my back. She called me and told me to rush down to the Board of Education building in downtown Brooklyn as soon as possible. Seems that Wingant High School, a Brooklyn school, had under-staffed themselves, and there was room for one more math teacher to fill a six month position. She told me where to go, what to do, and after I took what was called an Emergency Licensing Exam, I was hired. By the way, those exams basically tested whether your breath was warm, and you were alive. It was a very easy test, not really pushing me to any great *limits* (math teacher joke!).

So, I did what any red-blooded young man thirsting for a relationship with a girl would do. Much to my mom's dismay, I stayed in Brooklyn, moved in with Bob's old roommate, and now had money coming in to afford the rent. Mom went into retreat mode, literally disowning me for three months, and not a word was spoken between us. That was a hard thing to live through, but I knew that Sue was definitely worth the fight—she was my everything!

It is only fair to tell you that after time elapsed, mom and Sue became like mother and daughter. Mom loved Sue with all her heart, and Sue returned the feelings to mom. I had a tough time dealing with mom's antiquated way of thinking at first, but I certainly understood where she was coming from. That way of life was the way it was in old Italy, and habits and beliefs were very hard to change after a lifetime of thinking in one direction. But, I give mom great credit because she saw how Sue treated me with love and care. She saw how much I cared for Sue, and what a wonderful mother she eventually became to our children. Heck, she was a great cook as well… what else could an Italian mother want for her little boy? Mom realized, after time, that it's not what you are, it's who you are…what one is made of inside, not their religion or race. Their relationship evolved into a thing of beauty, respect, love, and fondness toward each other.

And now, back to our story! It was a beautiful, sunny day, and Sue and I made plans to go out to lunch. I hastily left my apartment, rode my ten speed bike down to the boardwalk entrance ramp, walked the vehicle up the ramp, and I was on my way. Admiring the scenic view of the Atlantic Ocean on my right and avoiding the pedestrians on the wooden walkway, I was in heaven, not a care in the world. I knew I was going to have a glorious day with Sue. So I was pedaling for fifteen minutes, just minding my own business when, suddenly, I heard a motorized scooter getting closer and closer to me. I turned my head around, and sure enough, it was a three-wheeled police van and it was aimed right for me. The officer, a seemingly nice fellow, stopped me and started asking me some questions. "Do you know what day it is? Are you aware of the rules of the boardwalk? Do you know that there should be no bicycles on the boardwalk today? Didn't you read the signs?" My answers to the cop were unfortunately delivered in a sarcastic manner, which didn't help my cause. You see, I was just doing my own thing, not thinking about anything else but going to spend the day with my girl. Why was he bothering me?

Apparently, Tuesdays were non-bike riding days on the boardwalk, which I was totally unaware of. I wasn't going to tell him that I had ridden on the boardwalk on previous Tuesdays as well. So, now it gets interesting. The officer asked me for my identification, license, credit card, anything. Remember I mentioned that I hastily left my apartment? Well the only paraphernalia I ran out of my place with was my keys to the front door. I had nothing. So he started to press me for information. Mistake number one: I gave him my correct name, address, and date of birth. He was feverishly scribbling it on what appeared to be a ticket. He filled out the rest of the citation and handed it to me. He started to motor off, at which point I flagged him down. "What do I do with this?" I asked. He informed me that I must appear in court at a particular day and hour. If not, in accordance with judicial procedures, there would be tremendous negative ramifications.

It was bad enough that I got a ticket for something as stupid as riding my bike on the boardwalk, but I now had to take a day to go to some cockamamie courtroom to take care of this! Why couldn't there be a fine amount written on the ticket instead? I'd pay it and call it a day.

I walked the bike to Sue's place the rest of the way for fear of being tabbed again. You know that feeling after you've been ticketed? Where you feel like every cop in New York is now watching your every move, so you'd better be extra careful? I related the whole ridiculous saga to Sue, and after she stopped laughing, her first comment to me was, "Why did you give him the correct information about yourself? You could have been your brother, Bob and let him handle it!" You know, she was absolutely right. What a dope! I could have been anyone I wanted to be, but no, I had a moment of weakness and decided to become "Honest Abe Lincoln!" How dumb was that? Actually, it would have been pretty funny to have taken on my brother's identity. Lord knows that I was constantly compared to him as a child growing up.

So, you would think that this epic tale was over, right? Well not exactly. The day came for my court appearance. Sue graciously accompanied me to the building located in downtown Brooklyn. The edifice had the appearance of a church, with hundreds of pew-like seats. In the front of the massive room was the judge's desk and chair. The first and most obvious thing to notice was that seated along with Sue and me were some very unsavory characters. Tough, weather-beaten faces, scarred with black, blue, and bloodied exteriors. We wanted out fast! So, the judge entered the confines, and the throng all stood en masse. We noticed that many in the crowd were handcuffed, shackled, and escorted by an officer. What were Sue and I doing here?

The courtroom barker started screaming out names and the reason for being there so that they could walk up and appear in front of the judge and plea their case. The names flowed and the convictions were read aloud—rape, killing, robbery, you name it, it was mentioned. Then my turn came up, my name was stated, and my reason for being here amongst these hardened criminals was told…riding his bike on the boardwalk! Sue and I were never so embarrassed in our lives. We actually saw stone-cold, granite-like faces turn to jelly as the criminals started to laugh so loud that some of the crowd had to be restrained and pulled aside just to let the proceedings continue. Find a rock and let Sue and me crawl under it, please. Mistake number two was about to take place. I took that long walk up to the judge's bench, all the while being laughed at with fingers pointed toward me. I heard comments like, "How's your tricycle?" and "What did you do, run someone over with your bike?" I made my way sheepishly up the aisle and tried to stay focused. Somewhere between being seated and the bench I got this great idea that I was going to plead guilty with an explanation. The judge heard my case, and directed me to make a second appearance to the courtroom a month later due to my type of plea. Before I could change my mind, I was ushered out of the building, now with a new court date in hand. Yeah, exactly what I needed to do, show up there again and face more ridicule…no way! Sue and I always got a belly-laugh chuckle out of this.

I guess I can say it now: its been so many years, a lifetime ago but because of expired statute of limitations, that second date came and went, followed by tons of notifications, and new dates to appear or else. Sue and I eventually got married, moved to a different locale, and the long arm of the law couldn't reach me any more. I avoided going into post offices for years for fear that my picture in profile with six numbers under the head shot was on the wall. I never liked my profile, anyway! So if my friendly neighborhood boardwalk officer or judge is still alive, I want you gentlemen to know that I am very willing to pay the fine for riding a bike on the boardwalk back in 1973!

Grandma Interruptus

I t was the summer of 1974, and Sue and I were officially engaged which started the period of disownment by my parents. Mom in particular was furious that I would not only date a Jewish girl, but then had the audacity to get engaged to her. Just stick the knife in mom's heart, and just for good measure, twist and turn it while it's in there. BLASPHEMOUS! SINFUL! IRREVERENT! You name it, I was all that in my mom's eyes. I guess I should have given back my choirboy robes to the church. I wouldn't be needing them anytime soon! I had no communication with mom for what seemed to be forever. I loved mom but I also loved Sue. I felt that I could keep both parties happy, but if push came to shove, Sue would win out. I was doing nothing wrong other than wanting to spend the rest of my life with the girl of my dreams. I guess any girl wouldn't have been good enough for mom's little boy, though. As I pointed out earlier in the book, mom and Sue's relationship eventually evolved into that of mother-daughter. In fact, they were even closer than mom and me. Sue was a great gal, and even though it took a lot of time and effort chipping away at mom's previous prejudice and ignorance brought over from the "old" country, their eventual closeness was a thing of beauty to witness.

The cold war lasted a good three months, but mom eventually acquiesced and called me. She saw how strong my feelings were for Sue, and she realized that she was to just about lose a son over this. The wedding date was so far in advance, mainly to give us time to gather up a priest to preside over the ceremony along with the rabbi that was already in place (I always joked with Sue that I would only get married to a girl with a masters degree so I needed to give her time to finish up her degree!). Do you know how hard it was to get a priest to leave his own parish on a Sunday, no less, and travel down to a catering hall? I went to my old church in Canarsie, Brooklyn to plead my case. I sat down with the priest that I had known since I was a kid. Who better to marry Sue and me? He gave me the "standard" church lines: Do you love her? Does she love you? Is she willing to sign a voucher stating that all children resulting from the marriage will be raised Catholic? Does she love you enough that she would convert to Catholicism? With that last query, I had had just about enough, and I arose from my seat and in a stern voice, told my "friendly" priest, "You know, I love Sue so much that I'm thinking of converting to Judaism!" And with that, I stormed out of his chambers never to return, ever!

Now I was in a deep bind. The one priest I had thought I could count on turned out to seemingly be working for mom. One day, though, Sue and I were walking around Bensonhurst, Brooklyn, and we passed by a "Reformed" Catholic Church. What did that mean? Did they re-form the structure of the building with all of the Sunday contributions parishioners so generously doled out? What did this exactly mean? We opened the massive wooden doors and walked in only to be greeted by a large imposing figure in priestly robes. "Can I help you both?" he asked. He seemed to be a nice fellow, tall and statuesque, but more importantly, willing to listen to us. We explained all of the difficulties that we had been having in trying to find a priest to attend and officiate at our wedding. To our surprise, there was no talk from the priest of conversions or of the religion of the future children; just talk of love, caring, and feelings. It was so refreshing to see a "man of the cloth" who saw our coming together as a positive thing; that we could learn from one another, take in the beauty of our differences in cultures as opposed to trying to mold ourselves into similarities. Differences enhanced our lives, not detracted from them. What idyllic, invigorating, energizing, exhilarating thoughts from a Catholic priest. This was our man!

Sue and I made an appointment with both the rabbi and the priest, just so everyone was on the same page for the wedding day. The key, in our minds, was that religion was not to be mentioned, or at least minimally at best. The ideas of love for one another, care, and compassion were the most important themes for Sue and me; not Jewish or Catholic, not pitting one God against another. We often thought that religions sometimes caused more harm than good. Think of all the conflicts in the world both in history and now that were and are presently fought over religion. Don't get me wrong, it certainly has its place, and Sue and I had nothing against those individuals we knew who were religious as long as they didn't push their beliefs on us. If it works for you, go for it. It just never worked for us, and that was one of the many reasons Sue and I fell for each other in the first place. By the way, the wedding went off without a hitch (pun intended), and everyone who attended thought it was handled by the two religious figures with dignity and class with an aura in the air, a sense of "divine" love and respect that Sue and I had for each other and each other's differences.

♈♈♈

Back to July of 1974. Sue and I had been affectionate and cuddly close, petting, stroking, caressing each other but we never did "it." Maybe it was because I had never been with a girl before and I was scared. Remember, I lived a very sheltered life under the wings of my parents in their apartment, and everything was so new to me. EVERYTHING! But the time was ripe. We had known each other for two years at this point. Sue had turned down an offer from her parents and her youngest sister to travel to California that summer. Just as I didn't move out to Shirley in Suffolk County so I could stay in Brooklyn to be close to her, she chose not to leave the east coast of the United States to be with me. We had an entire, glorious summer to look forward to.

Ready for the "Jackie Collins" portion of the book? Now Sue lived in Brighton Beach, a block away from her two grandmothers and cousins—important facts to recall later on in this saga. We decided that today was the day. Yes, the juices were flowing and the time was now…all systems go, Houston! Sue reassured me that all would be fine and that she would help me. Something told me that I was going to need a lot of help. My heart started racing when Sue took my hand. She led me into her parent's bedroom. The coast was clear because her parents were on the other side of the United States! So we ambled onto Sue's parent's bed. We started to kiss and hug passionately as we had done before. Sue unbuttoned my shirt, and I undid her blouse. She was wearing short-shorts that had four snaps in the front. Those were real sexy and so was Sue. We were finally down to our undergarments, and then finally to skin. We had been at this stage before, but never beyond. Wow, she looked great. She always looked great, but with the anticipation of the event, Sue was particularly beautiful. Our bodies intertwined, my face buried in Sue's chest, and we were one, almost! The setting was right, the feelings were high, the blood was pumping, and we were ready for lift-off!

Just then, *knock, knock, knock,* followed the doorbell ringing. WHAT??? You've got to be kidding. Houston, we have a problem! Just when the old retro rocket was to fire up for entry into uncharted space!

We froze, silent and motionless. "Susan, Susan, are you in there?" Oy vey, it was Sue's grandmother. Sue knew her grandmother had the front door key and she would come in if Sue didn't respond. What were we to do, naked babes in each other's arms, scrambling to fit one leg in the correct pant leg at a time, buttoning our respective clothes at the speed of light. Quickly wasn't fast enough. We needed it done yesterday!

Sue yelled out, "Yes Grandma, I'll be there in a minute." Of course, it would not have looked too good if I was there anywhere in the apartment, let alone the bedroom all disheveled and sweaty. I couldn't hide in any closets—there was no space—and I couldn't fit under the bed.

I did the only thing I could. I climbed out of the bedroom window, probably semi-dressed, onto the fire escape and started a descent downward, tripping, clanking, missing steps, bumbling, and stumbling all the way. Sue, in the meantime, answered the door calmly and efficiently. "Hello Grandma. How are you?" Grandma answered her back, pacing through the apartment as if she had this sixth sense, expecting to see something (or someone) unusual. The inspection was over, and satisfied that everything was in order, Grandma made small talk with Sue, while rummaging through the sparsely filled refrigerator shelves. Sue, all the while, is hoping that I made it safely down the rusty old steps of the building's fire escape. Grandma ended up staying for a good hour, just asking questions, munching on some toast, and drinking some orange juice.

I was now downstairs waiting for some sign, some

"coast is clear" signal, but it never came. So I took it upon myself to make an unexpected visit. I traveled in a more conventional way, up the elevator to the fourth floor and rang the apartment bell. Sue answered the door stating, "Grandma, Joe's here visiting." I came in to the kitchen, and cool as a cucumber and slick as a grease spill, I greeted Grandma as I would have if it were "normal" conditions. "How nice to see you, Joe; where have you been recently?" "Well Grandma, I'm studying hard so I can climb up the ladder of success!" We all talked for a good long time. She mentioned the recent art museums that she visited and told Sue and me about the Paul Gauguin exhibit she saw recently at the Metropolitan Museum of Art in Manhattan. Grandma, almost taunting us, goes on to describe the naked Tahitian women that were the subjects of many of Gauguin's paintings...come on, that's hitting below the belt, literally! Why couldn't she have seen Salvador Dali, or Picasso...no naked women there! This entire episode started out as a sexual fantasy and instead became all too surreal. Sue and I were hoping that Grandma would do a Van "Go" quickly but that wasn't happening!

The three of us had a nice time chatting and passing the time together, while my erotic genes were erupting inside of me. At some point, Sue's grandmother mentioned that my voice seemed a little higher pitched than usual. "It's the salt air here in Brighton Beach...affects my vocal chords all the time!" All right, Grandma, you made your point, all too clear!

Excuse the expression, but the best-laid plans of mice and men often go awry! A couple of things were obvious to both Sue and me. First, Grandma had a mission to accomplish while the rest of the family was in California, and even though she couldn't tail Sue and me 24/7, NOTHING was going to happen on HER watch. Secondly, this just wasn't going to be the day…mission aborted, Houston!

So you probably want to know when the "day" was and what were the details. Well I'm going to do to you readers what Grandma did to me…leave you hanging!

Our Wedding

Sue and I wanted a summer wedding, and as we always tried, we also wanted to accommodate as many friends and family as possible. We knew that holding a wedding later in the summer wouldn't be good as most of our friends were teachers, and they had already made their summer vacation plans. Having it earlier in June wasn't the greatest either. With final exams and Regents being given, weekends needed to be spent marking papers, not dancing across a ballroom floor. So it came down to June 27, 1976 or July 4, 1976.

The styles of tuxedos being shown around the time of July 4th were incredibly hokey. I actually tried on a red, white, and blue tuxedo with a star-studded puffy shirt and a cummerbund that represented the flag. We knew that our wedding was important, but we also knew not to compete with America's birthday. I had inner fears that instead of picking Sue and me up in chairs and dancing around with us on the dance floor, the wedding entourage would hoist and scale me up the nearest flagpole! We also didn't want our first dance to be to the tune of "The Star-Spangled Banner." Truly, it didn't take much to convince us to wed on June 27th, particularly after trying on that tuxedo! So Sue and I had a great time at our wedding and a week later America got its chance to enjoy its own spotlight and feast over its 200 years of freedom.

Some friends of mine made the point of reminding me that by getting married, I just lost my freedom! They were kidding, of course. I relished the chance to share my life with Sue, my love. We were captivated by each other's charm and grace, and all we saw, especially both being math teachers, was that the whole was greater than its parts. Our union (to coin another math term) was so special, and we both looked forward to many, many years to come.

Our wedding was like Charles and Diana's, but on a smaller scale...much smaller. For Sue and me, it was a storybook wedding that played out in real life. We were surrounded by friends and family who were so happy for us. I remember discussing with Sue, in amazement, about the number of people who truly cared about us, and our happiness, as they clanged their goblets with their forks and spoons to get a look at us smooching. I encouraged the clanging, at one point leading the charge myself. What the heck, I went into the kitchen to get extra silverware to hand out to the entourage just so I could kiss Sue over and over again throughout the reception celebration!

In preparation for the wedding, though, I desperately needed a foot operation. I was born with two left feet, if you know what I mean. I couldn't dance to save my life. Sue, on the other hand, could hold her own on the dance floor, well enough to get by. That was the level where I wanted to be. We enrolled in an adult education class in a local high school, where every Friday night, we learned—or tried to learn—the fox trot, the hustle, the cha-cha-cha, and other formal dances to get me though the reception. It was a torturous two hours but it had to be done!

At the end of the ten sessions, I think I knew as much as I had before I signed up for the class. One dance step flowed into another. I would say that it was a success because I never fell down or got my feet tangled up with Sue's. It also made for a very cheap Friday night date!

Interestingly, Sue and I were both fans of John Denver songs. One of his nicest tunes was "Annie's Song." You know the one that talks about "filling up senses like a night in the forest." The words were beautiful, and most importantly, it was a song that I could possibly dance to. This was all well and good if I were marrying a girl named Annie, but since I was marrying a woman named Sue, we had to scrap the

John Denver song and go to plan B. Another very influential group back then was The Beatles. Both Sue and I loved their music. Sue had told me she wanted desperately to get to Shea Stadium in 1964 when they came to America—she and 100 million other screaming teens. She never quite made it there, but her love for their music never waned. We picked the beautiful ballad, "And I Love Her" as our wedding song and first dance. It was great as we both shuffled across the dance floor and the throng applauded. I took that to mean that they were happy that we didn't land *on* the floor! I couldn't wait until the bandleader announced for everyone to join the happy couple on the floor. Once we were surrounded by great numbers of people, I felt like we had made it. Now I could let my Beatle haircut down and really dance like Arthur and Katherine Murray, like Fred and Ginger (only kidding)! All in all, it was a day to remember. People who even weren't in attendance said they were there and still talk about it! I guess we actually must have had as many people as Charles and Diana!

That evening after the wedding, Sue and I lay prone on the bed while we were scooping up all of the wedding checks, flipping them in the air as if we had hit the lottery. That was a little difficult to do with the three pressure cookers we received as gifts! The best gift, however, was that we had each other, and we looked to the future with great hope and promise. We felt that when two people cared and loved each other as much as we did, *nothing* could stop us. To us, our wedding vows meant *forever*...

I, Joe, take you Sue, to be my wife, to have and to hold from this day forward, for better or for worse, for richer, for poorer, in sickness and in health, to love and to cherish from this day forward until death do us part.

Forever. When you are as "young and foolish" as Sue and I were at that time, you don't see the possibilities, the hardships, and the tragedies that life sometimes burdens you with. I guess that's true for any young couple starting out. All we saw was that we were starting a brand new, wonderful phase of our lives called "marriage," and we were going to live it to the fullest. And why not? Things couldn't have looked any better back in 1976. And live it, we did.

Our Early Married Life Together

We took trips, saw concerts in the park, camped out in remote places in the Adirondacks, biked, played tennis, and attended sporting events. And that was just the first day! But seriously, we were like two little kids whose parents had just set them free, and we took full advantage of our newly found freedom. One night, we realized that it was all right to order a pizza at midnight if we wanted to—who was going to stop us? We would deal with the bellyaches by ourselves if necessary. Marriage, for me, was as close to heaven on earth as it could be. I was with the one person I loved dearly, and I wanted to spend as much time with her as possible. Sue felt the same way. We were a pair of aces, a match that couldn't be beat.

We did it up for seven years before Matthew, our firstborn, came along. We took two flights to the "left" (west) coast during that time. The first was a camping flight. We packed all of our gear from tent to propane stove to sleeping bags. This was my first time on a jet so the experience was new and exciting. We landed in San Francisco, where we stayed two nights at a plush hotel. I can't tell you the name of the place for fear of repercussions. Sue and I learned rather quickly that California—in particular, the Bay Area—could get cold at nights, something we were not prepared for. So, being "young and foolish," we purloined a blanket from that hotel, and it became very handy throughout the rest of the camping portion of the trip. We saw Big Sur, Yosemite National Park, the giant redwoods, and also visited with friends that lived in California.

My brother happened to be out there at this time as well. He was visiting a friend who was learning to be a translator at the Monterey Institute of International Studies. Sue and I were invited to stay the night in this home, right off campus, where prospective translators from all over the world were rooming. We graciously said yes—the thought of a real bed as opposed to a bed of gravel was a "no-brainer"! The house had all the amenities that campsites don't afford you, and I decided to take a real bath in a luxurious tub. Unfortunately, I forgot to lock the door, and much to my surprise, a geisha girl walked in on me while I was scrubbing away! I didn't know whether or not to get up and bow or just turn as beet-red as the color of her kimono. She ran out, I sank further under the water level, and both of us never made any further eye contact for the rest of the visit. It was embarrassing, especially when I tried to explain it to Sue! In true Sue form, she had a good laugh over it and then moved on. How I wished it had been Sue instead of the geisha!

The rest of the trip took Sue and me to places north of Sacramento, to a city named Yuba City, and as far down south as Anaheim to visit Disneyland. I had a friend who lived in Yuba City. Lew was an old friend from my childhood days, and after he graduated from high school, he entered the Air Force. He married a wonderful girl, Trina, while he was stationed out west. Sue and I had never met Trina, but just as Lew had described her in his letters, she was as friendly as could be. We made it to their house in Yuba City where Trina informed us that Lew was coming in from Okinawa just that evening. What timing and what amazing good luck. We drove to the Air Force base and waited on the tarmac as the huge plane pulled up. Now, mind you, Lew, being stationed overseas, hadn't seen Trina for months. The stairway was lowered and out came the soldiers running to greet their loved ones. We saw Lew as he raced down the stairs, ran towards us, and then planted a big kiss on *my* cheek. That's right, MY cheek! He was so surprised to see me and Sue, he completely forgot about Trina! Lew had a lot of explaining to do with his Air Force buddies over that one!

Sue and I had a wonderful time reminiscing about the good old days as well as the days to come. Trina was pregnant with their first child, so Sue talked a lot to her about it. Sue admitted later that she learned how to parent because she emulated Trina and her techniques. We had the chance to thank Trina years later after our two sons, Matthew and Justin were born, not because they were our kids but because they turned out to be the most loving, caring, and sensitive children. Sue's adaptation of Trina's nurturing was part of the reason why.

𝓡𝓡𝓡

Sue was destined to be a great mother. She put everything aside to raise the kids and mold them into fine upstanding men. She taught high school math for ten years in a school where kids and the surrounding area were downtrodden. Many of her students didn't even know who their parents were. Because of this experience, Sue became a full time mom. It truly made a difference for her to be home and be there for the boys. She could have continued to do great things, influencing her students in the positive ways she did, but it was now time for her to devote her full attention and love to our guys. I could tell from the get-go that Sue would be an outstanding parent. All I had to do was see how her students loved and adored her. She was a surrogate mother to those kids. She received tons of accolades from the students; things like you're the best teacher ever or thanks for caring about us. She would come home at the beginning of Christmas vacation with loads of gifts, many of them handmade by her economically deprived students. Yes, she was a natural at caring and nurturing. Sue always knew the right thing to say when Matthew or Justin was feeling down or hurt. She could always relieve the tension with some deflecting tactic. Sue made life fun for the kids, and they sensed it and appreciated her for it. She always knew how to turn their frowns into smiles. I could never match her skill as a parent, and I felt so fortunate that the kids had her there. I would also, deep down inside, be terrified if for whatever reason, she couldn't be there for the boys. They loved her so much. It's not that the kids didn't like or love me, but they had the type of bond that only sons and mothers could have. I have that bond, to this day, with my mom. It is the kind of connection that psychologists write about. I knew the kids were in great hands with Sue around.

♌♌♌

The rest of the trip was spent enjoying each other's company as we drove down the coast of California. If you get the chance, you must see the seventeen-mile drive around Monterrey and Carmel. It was breath-taking, and Sue and I truly appreciated its beauty. In a car with the girl you love, driving around amongst all of this grandeur and splendor, it couldn't have been any better. It was what life should have been like every day and not just for a couple of weeks on vacation.

We were also able to learn a lot about each other on that trip. It was, after all, the first time that we had spent that much time alone together. Sue learned how frugal I was—which sounds better than calling myself cheap—when I made the decision to rent a canary yellow Capri mini-car for the trip without air conditioning, just so we could save a few bucks.

And I do mean a few; it wouldn't have broken the bank to get the AC. I didn't hear the end of it from her, and rightfully so, when Sue contracted a urinary tract infection because it was so hot in the car and she was sweating profusely! That one event changed me. I realized that we had a partnership, and it was ever so important to understand and listen to my mate and consider her feelings. She was always like that toward me, but this trip magnified what I already knew about Sue. I think I became a better husband to Sue because of this one incident.

Our second trip to California was another great experience in seeing the beauty of our United States. The unfortunate part of the trip happened during our flight home. We were over Ohio, in particular, Cleveland. I was a white-knuckle traveler to begin with, but I turned ashen when the jet seemingly dropped hundreds of feet down. We were passing through a thunderstorm, and the turbulence was frightening. Sue always told people that I was making this part of the story up, but for me, it was real. I was prepared to go down and die, but I just didn't want to die over Cleveland. As it says on W.C. Fields' gravestone, I'd rather be in Philadelphia. I didn't want to be there either, but certainly not Cleveland! (There go all of my potential sales for this book from the greater Cleveland area!) I'm not a religious person by any stretch of the imagination, but I did take this as some kind of sign, and to this day, I have kept my feet on the ground. Sue, being Sue showing concern for her mate, didn't mind. If we were to take any future trips, we would be doing it by car.

Pyramid Visit

I t's early 1977, and Sue and I were now married for less than one year. She graduated Brooklyn College in four years, took her New York State Math Licensing Certification Exam, and promptly landed a teaching job. My story was just a tad different. You see a little event was occurring across the globe that scared the heck out of me. The Vietnam War was in full force and since it was probably the first war that was on our television sets each night at dinnertime, I saw that I wanted no part of it. I was a lover, not a fighter! The last gun I toted was as a child; a toy Winchester rifle that shot air caps. I wouldn't have known which end of the weapon was up. This was certainly something to avoid. At the time, the United States government was not drafting boys that had either a medical problem (punctured eardrum, flat feet, etc) or a 2-S deferment. 2-S meant that you were a full time student in college. Well, I didn't meet the first requirement.

Unfortunately, I was as healthy as the proverbial horse (even though I had some friends who poked holes in their ear drums just to get out of conscription). I didn't know anyone in Canada—many boys were escaping to the north to seek political asylum. It was too cold up there, and it would have been one heck of a daily commute for Sue to go to work!

So the 2-S deferment was the answer. I stayed in Brooklyn College one semester longer so I eventually graduated in four and a half years. That made a major difference in my life. First of all it kept me from wearing army fatigues in Vietnam, and two, it kept me from getting a job. You see, little to my knowledge, New York City was having such financial difficulties at the time and they put a freeze on administering the Math Licensing exam. Here I was, ready to take my place among the pantheon of great, new, up and coming teachers, but New York City was not ready for me.

The exam was reissued, and I passed it with flying colors so one hurdle was overcome. Next, I needed a position to open up for me. Surely, there must have been some old math teacher ready for the pasture. I bided my time, hopeful that I would be hired some time soon, as Sue all the while dutifully got up every morning to traipse into work. I got up with her, made her breakfast and a bagged lunch, kissed her, and saw her off every morning. I made my weekly phone call to the Brooklyn College Placement Center to see if a job was open. It got to be comical—every Monday morning at ten, I'd make my call. The secretary manning the phone knew it had to be me on the other end, and all he would say is "yes" or "no." There was no need for pleasantries at that point, just "yes" or "no." After multitudes of weekly rejections, I got very frustrated. My day was mapped out—back to bed to dream about a math teaching job, after saying good bye to Sue, until my favorite soap opera, *All My Children,* came on television. A lot of drama was being played out both on the show, as well as in my own life. Do you know how hard it was to see your newly wedded wife going to a job, bringing money to our household, with me idle around the place contributing no salary, no nothing? I learned a lot about myself in that period of time. I thought that I was above the macho, Italian upbringing that states that the man was the bread winner, and the wife was there to cook, clean, and occasionally remain barefoot and pregnant! Apparently, I was molded and brain-washed by my parents more than I'd thought. Mind you, I didn't want to stop Sue from working. I just desperately needed to pull my own weight, making some kind of fertile contribution to the household.

What does a person in my position do to solve the dilemma? He goes on a game show, what else? The afternoon television viewing was starting to appeal to me; in particular, the game shows. At the time, there were some shows originating in New York City and lots more from California. Scratch those, especially due to my fear of flying. One game in particular that intrigued me was produced and taped on Columbus Circle and Seventh Avenue in Manhattan—the *$10,000 Pyramid*, hosted by Dick Clark. Sue saw my obsession with this crazy idea, so she went out and purchased the home version of the Pyramid. Every night, come hell or high water, we played the game after dinner. Sue and I actually got fairly good at it. I saw that I was best at giving the clues as opposed to receiving them. I jumped in the air every time when we "beat" the buzzer, and I just knew that this enthusiasm was going to propel me on to the show.

I went down to the studio and filled out an application, along with the hundreds of other potential contestants. Looking at the men in the group, I wondered how many of them were here because of my reasons. I was finally going to pull my weight and win big money. Truth was, back in the 70s, starting teachers were making around $9,500 a year, and I was thinking, I could make that and more in one show! The applicants were ushered into a room where we paired off as partners and played the game under the watchful eye of the producer of the show. It was a mixed feeling playing with someone who actually was vying for your stardom, your cash. Nevertheless, we played and played and played for hours. Finally, came decision time. You either got a thumbs up or down from the show's hierarchy. I screamed and jumped a mile high when I was told, YES...they wanted me, I fit their contestant mold. I was in seventh heaven coming home on the subway that afternoon. Sue and I rejoiced with a special meal, and of course, more home game playing.

The day came for the taping of the show to be aired in the future. The celebrities were exactly who a game player would want, Ann Meara and Nipsey Russell. It couldn't get any better than that. These stars actually cared for the contestant, trying above and beyond to win for them. The day was looking good. Sue took off from work that day to give me support and rode the subway with me to the studio. When we got there, we noticed that there were more contestants than was needed for the week's worth of taping, so right away I saw that being there guaranteed nothing. We again were ushered into the "warm-up" room. For whatever reason, maybe pressure, maybe expectations, maybe nerves, I just didn't have it. I stunk during practice, and I just knew this was not to be my day.

The way it worked was that five shows were taped in one sitting so the celebrities did their appearance and were done. Ever notice that the contestants who make it on the next day's show are still wearing the same clothes, but the stars get to change? The selection of the order of appearances for us was solely based on how we performed in warm-ups. The best people, most liveliest, most enthusiastic, most crazy got to go on toward the beginning of the week's tapings; the less versed went toward the middle to back end of the week's taping. That day, I didn't get called at all. I was so disappointed; all my friends, my family, and of course Sue were expecting great things and got nothing.

Weeks passed by and no phone calls came from the Pyramid to ask me back for a second chance. I kept thinking that I was good enough to get called to be on the show before, why couldn't they let me try just one more time? I got up enough nerve and I called the show. A secretary gave me the line that they were sorry that it didn't work, try another game show. But I was determined to convince her to give me one more shot. Somehow, I did just that. There was new hope and new life in these once rejected bones.

I guess, sometimes, when it rains it pours. A week before the taping, I continued to call my Brooklyn College Placement contact. That Monday, he said that there was a job in Nassau County in a small town high school, and reluctantly, he gave me the information about the school district and the job description. He didn't think it was what I was looking for. I took the facts down and set up an interview with the chairman of the high school math department. I impressed them so much that I was hired on the spot. I was to start in a month. The Pyramid was just icing on the cake.

Maybe it was the security of knowing I had a glorious job awaiting me, or maybe I felt more comfortable being at the studio again. For whatever reason, I got on the show; a Thursday airing (back end of the week), but on television none the less. Sue wanted to accompany me again, but I suggested that she not attend. Maybe I felt a little more pressure with her seated in the audience. Maybe I didn't want to potentially disappoint her again if I wasn't selected. Whatever the reason, I figured I'd come home with some glorious news and eventually we could both see the taped show on television when it was to be aired finally. Reluctantly, she went to work that morning and waited for my triumphant return later in the afternoon. My stars for that week were Carol Ita White and Ron Glass. You would probably know Glass better because of his role on *Barney Miller*, but who was Carol Ita White? She played "Big" Rosy, a one season character on *Laverne and Shirley*. I had no idea who she was seeing that I never really watched *Laverne and Shirley*. Her father was more recognizable, Jesse White—the lonely Maytag repairman!

Contestants on the show were interrogated prior to taping to find out what information would go on Dick Clark's index card. With me, it was either the teaching thing or the marriage thing. They told me that they had too many teachers on that week, so for me, they focused on the marriage thing. I didn't mind if Sue got some play on television as well! With that, the show started and I was introduced by my good "old" buddy, Dick. "So, Joe, it says here that you're a newlywed" to which I nervously respond, "That's right Dick...a *new* newlywed." Enough idle banter... let the games begin...I'm matched up with Carol in the first round, and boy was I ever lucky. She was a great player answering all of my very confusing clues. She pulled responses out of thin air and saved me.

We won the game, and it was time to go the winner's circle. Carol gave me great clues, terrific ones at that. First Square, she said, "Gin and tonic, screwdriver, seven and seven," and I, not being a drinker, responded with the answer "drinks." That was not enough for the powers that be...they wanted "mixed drinks" or "alcoholic drinks" Strike one. But to her credit, Carol moved on, the clock ticking away, and we proceeded to get the next squares on the big board..."Alfred Hitchcock movies", "things a candle would say", "things that have branches", and "things you invest in". The one that drove me up a wall was the second one..."things that lay eggs". Carol's clues were right on the money and my answers

53

were sharp and crisp, but I just wasn't thinking about laying eggs. So I walked away with $400 and moved on to work with Mr. Glass.

Now Ron was, at best, a mediocre player who appeared like he wanted to be anywhere but there playing a stupid game that he seemingly could care less about. Well, needless to say, you take a mediocre player in Mr. Glass and a "Thursday" contestant such as myself, and we stunk up the joint. Oh, was it bad…so bad that Carol actually felt sorry for me. As she was escorting her new winning partner to the big board, she turned to me, waved and mouthed, "I'm sorry!" How's that for dedication to your former partner. To this day, I think she really liked me (I could let my male ego soar occasionally, okay?).

I was on my way home on the subway train, talking to myself, making all sorts of gyrations with my arms and hands. Why didn't I say, "Things that lay eggs"? Apparently, I was screaming it loud enough that other riders on the train gave me plenty of room for fear that I would explode. I must have looked like a crazed person, angry and talking out aloud to myself! All in all, for a couple hours of "work," I came home with $400 in cash and $250 dollars in the ever so famous "consolation" prizes.

Sue and I were both employed now, and all was right with the world. Every day was a great surprise, though, because delivered in front of our entryway door to our apartment was another consolation prize. One day we came home to find hundreds of boxes of Fab detergent piled as high as the door. Another day came the Richardson's After-Dinner Mints followed by loads of cheeses, thirty bottles of Blue Lustre Carpet Shampoo, and a carpet cleaning machine. Unfortunately, Sue and I had no carpets in our tiny little apartment. I ended up using it as hair shampoo instead...(only kidding!). It was a blast receiving all of this stuff.

Remember, I mentioned that I had just been hired by the Parkland school district. This tiny, but affluent, community was terrific. By the time the show was to air, I already had a month of teaching under my belt. One day in passing, I mentioned to one of my students that I'd be on television tomorrow. Good kid that he was, the student told his dad about my appearance, so he loaded up his Beta-max recording machine to start recording the show at 2 p.m. sharp. Years later, Sue's dad converted the tape to VHS, so I actually have a video record of my Andy Warhol "15 minutes of fame." I am so glad I mentioned the air date to that student...he got an "A" of course!

One last thought about game shows and the celebrities that go on them. This actually occurred many years after my television "gig." The *New York Daily News* once took a poll and ran the results in the paper. The article was entitled, "Which star would you want to be on a game show with, and which are ones to avoid." Which star was voted to be best team player? People like Ann Meara, Nipsey Russell, Soupy Sales, Tony Randall, Billy Crystal, and so on. But more importantly—ready for this? Ahh, retribution at last...I kid you not—the star that most contestants did not want on their team was Mr. Ron Glass, number one offender! Boy this made me feel vindicated for the second half of my one and only Pyramid appearance!

"Typhoid" Susan

D o you recall the true story of "Typhoid" Mary Mallon?
Mary was the first person in America to be identified as
a health carrier of typhoid fever in the late 1800s/early
1900s. Her mother had typhoid fever during her pregnancy,
and Mary was born with the disease. Mary, the human carrier,
was a healthy person who had the typhoid bacteria in her body
but was able to survive without being felled herself by the
infection. She was a cook and she infected forty-seven people,
three of whom died from typhoid. She caused a lot of damage
to many other unsuspecting innocent people. She initially had
no knowledge that she was the cause of the spread of typhoid.
Her notoriety occurred later when she vehemently denied her
own role in spreading the disease, together with her refusal to
cease working as a cook. She was forcibly quarantined twice
by public health authorities and died in quarantine.

So how in the world does "Typhoid Mary" possibly

relate to Sue? Well, first of all, the severity of our situation wasn't anywhere close to Mary's. As a matter of fact, the saga I'm about to tell you is quite amusing.

The epic tale takes place back in the early 1980s in New Jersey. Sue's oldest sister, Lynn, lived in Jersey during the infestation period of gypsy moths. Those were the insects that would climb up the bark and stems of trees and bushes in the evening, feed on all of the green leaves and foliage they could find, then when sated, would climb back down to digest their pillage. Now I'm not going to tell you that these little buggers were hungry, but did you ever hear of the Sahara Forest? Of course not. The moths sapped all the life out of the trees and transformed the area into arid, barren land. You may know it by its present name…the Sahara Desert! These guys could change the look of a once healthy arboretum into a dry wasteland just to satisfy their insatiable need to fill their bellies!

Lynn had a lot of good, fertile Jersey firewood in her backyard that she really had no use for. Knowing that Sue and I had just installed a brand new, gorgeous fireplace in our den, she offered the wood to us. Sue thanked her sister gratefully and accepted the generous offer. After all, fireplace wood was quite expensive to purchase, so why not?

We needed some means to transport the cords of wood. I asked my brother, Bob, who just happened to own a big telephone service van. Bob purchased it because, in addition to his day job as teacher, he was moonlighting as a disco dancer/DJ for parties and such at night. He needed a fairly good-sized van to house his turntables, rotating disco light ball, and his humongous amplifiers. He was a real life *Saturday Night Fever* "John Travolta" after the sun set, playing pop music and getting people on the dance floor. He was quite good at what he did, but the economy wasn't so good to him. Since business was slow, he allowed me to use the truck to haul some timber.

Sue and I drove to Jersey and piled the van with wood to the point that you couldn't see out of the back windows. Sue and I barely fit in the spacious truck with our newly gained cut trunks of fresh Jersey trees. Now, I tended to be a procrastinator, and seeing that Bob didn't need the van any time soon, I parked on the curb near our house. We picked up the wood in October, and the van lay silent with its contents until May of the next year. Now that's the epitome of procrastination!

One day toward the end of May, Sue's cousin, Ian, was visiting us, and he decided to walk down our block and take in its tree-lined splendor. He came running back and summoned me out to take a look at something he thought to be peculiar. He led me to the parked van and he instructed me to peer through the passenger side window. To my utter surprise, I couldn't see through to the driver's side window. Why, you may ask? There were millions and millions of web-like strings hanging from the inside roof of the van and attached to the strings were thousands of larvae. They had formed a dense "wall" of solid silk webs. It was unbelievable. Apparently, the wood that we had taken from New Jersey was infested with gypsy moth eggs waiting to hatch. Sue and I had provided the perfect medium for these buggers to "uncocoon" themselves. The inside of the van was dark, a bit moist, and hot as we approached the summer months and these guys couldn't have had a better place to enter into this world!

I called to Sue, and after her initial shock, she told me in a hysterical voice to just drive it off the nearest cliff I could find. I assumed that she meant with me in it! She was not a happy camper. After some heavy deliberation with her, we decided that number one, there are no cliffs near us (thank goodness for that!), and two, if there was a mountainous area near us, it would do the environment no good anyway. So, we came up with the bright idea that we would "bomb" the van—insect bomb that is.

The next day, I purchased three heavy duty, grenade-shaped insect repellents. I dressed up in overalls, gloves, a ski mask, goggles, and boots and was ready to do my best "Rambo" impersonation. Sue, at my signal, swung open the back doors of the truck, and I pulled the pins and in the same motion, I flung two grenades into the back of the garbled, tangled silk webs. We repeated the process by the front passenger door. We had to time this just so because we certainly wanted to keep the moths contained in Bob's once pristine van. By now, all of our neighbors thought that we had lost it and 911 psychiatric help was surely on its way.

We retreated to the comfort of our home and reflected on the events of the day and the events that led us to this day. After a restless sleep, it was morning and time to witness the carnage in the van—hopefully. I am happy to report that the debugging mission was a success. They apparently had no chance. There they were, lying belly up with their little legs and antennas facing upward, motionless and, more importantly, lifeless. We wiped out an entire civilization of potentially harmful tree eaters. Our street, our community, our town was safe from the foliage feeders. We were fully expecting the town to throw a parade in our honor for saving our green community. Then we came back to reality and remembered that we were the ones who brought the moths here in the first place.

Today, "Typhoid Mary" is a generic term for a carrier of a dangerous disease who is a danger to the public because of refusal to take appropriate precautions. So you see, this was truly a case of "Typhoid" Susan, or should I say, "Gypsy Moth" Susan! We, akin to "Typhoid Mary", had no idea that we were about to cause the largest defoliation in an area since the United States used Agent Orange in Vietnam! But as they say, "All's well that ends well!" Once the coast was clear to get into the van, I brought my trusty Electrolux vacuum to the curb and painstakingly cleaned every single stinking piece of wood making sure no remnants of bug larva were still in hiding. I then piled the wood into stacks in our backyard where I wanted them to be eight months ago, and then proceeded to clean, polish, and refurbish Bob's van so that it was driven back to him in better condition than when Sue and I borrowed it. He was totally unaware of this whole episode until I eventually told him about it years later.

So let's take inventory here. Think about it for a minute—if I had been prompt at taking the logs out and piling them into cords in the backyard in October, I would have been unknowingly opening up Pandora's Box, freeing the moths to the greenery of our town. Instead, by waiting a good amount of time, I smartly allowed the moths to hatch in a very controlled and sealed environment, namely Bob's van! How bright was that of me—totally planned and thought out precisely. It's difficult to type when one of your arms is patting yourself on your back! I guess the two morals of the story are that it's absolutely correct to procrastinate and secondly, *never look a gift log in its moth!* From that day on, Sue and I could never complain about our kids not doing their homework assignments in a timely fashion anymore! Start procrastinating…NOW!

The Birth
of Our Children

nother great joy in our lives was our children, Matthew and Justin. They, too, have connections between them, other than the fact that they are brothers. The story goes like this…being math teachers, Sue and I obviously calculated things all of the time. We actually multiplied twice in our lives! She and I went to all of the Lamaze classes in preparation for the birth of our first child. We kept up on all of the doctor appointments making sure that this would be a picture-perfect birth. Sue had a sonogram done so that we could see the fetus, though those old sonogram machines didn't have the capabilities of today's technology. I always thought that that first picture looked like a wiped windshield of a car while driving through a rainstorm. Those of you who had babies in the 80s know exactly what I'm talking about! Somehow, however, the doctor was able to tell us the baby was fine and all was well. As it turned out, though, the baby's due date was twelve days earlier than expected. Now this couldn't have worked out any better for me. You see, the regular school year ended on June 24, 1983, and summer school, which I taught annually was to start on July 5, 1983. When Sue's water broke (a term I still have trouble envisioning), we quickly got all of the materials (a can of tennis balls, ice chips, towels, etc.) that the Lamaze teacher mentioned to bring, and we traveled to the hospital. This was not a Lucille Ball television episode, but instead, we were calm and collected considering it was to be our first child. Within hours, at 9:44 p.m. on June 30, 1983, a healthy, baby boy was introduced to the world. His name was Matthew, partially due to his parents' connection to the subject of math. Being that I am a math teacher and not an English teacher, Matthew's middle name had to be something that I could spell. Sue and I both liked the name Brian, however I knew that if we spelled it conventionally, half the time I'd be writing "Brain" instead, so we compromised and spelled it Bryan. I knew I was fairly safe with that! As it turned out, Brain wouldn't have been so bad. Matthew went on to be valedictorian of his high school, graduated from Princeton University with high honors, and is presently working on his PhD in Mathematics at Berkeley. So Matthew probably realized that he had lots to do, decided that he spent enough time in Sue's womb, wanted to get into his own womb— I mean room—and he hit the earth running and hasn't stopped yet.

Remember I mentioned a connection between Matthew and Justin at the start of this chapter. Well, Sue and I were faced with a similar predicament five years later. We wanted Matthew to have a sibling, but once again due to time restraints dealing with school (regular school and summer school), we needed careful planning. Justin was due somewhere around the date of Matthew's birthday, but apparently was to a bit late, eleven days to be precise. The date was June 29, 1988, a day before Matthew's birthday. Sue and I were shopping at a pool store to buy a twelve-foot above ground pool for his birthday the next day. I don't know if it was the sound of the pool water, the filters pumping, or the circulating water throughout the dozens of display models, but it happened. Sue's water broke, and this time it was like Lucy getting to the hospital to have Little Ricky. Have you ever tried driving on the Long Island Expressway at four or five in the afternoon? There is a reason that roadway is referred to as the world's largest parking lot. I was tempted to violate some road rule just so I could attract a friendly police car. This way we could have gotten a great escort to the hospital.

As it turns out, we got there, the hospital staff supplied us with a room, and the monitors were put in place. Hours passed by and nothing happened. We were asked to take a walk around the hospital grounds to help induce labor. Again, nothing eventful occurred. It is now approaching midnight, and still, no activity. By the way, we didn't forget our Matthew through all of this confusion. That would truly have made this a "Virtual Lucy" episode. He was having a play date with a friend while Sue and I were pool shopping. Seeing that we had to rush over to the hospital, we asked our sister-in-law to pick him up and have him sleep over that night with his cousin.

To make a short story long, at 1:55 a.m. on the date of June 30th, Justin arrived in the world. That's right, you read it correctly, June 30th. The kids share the same birthday. Would you like to know the odds of that happening? After all, Sue and I are math teachers and could whip out that answer in a heartbeat (1 in 365)! Do you realize that a difference of two hours, either for Matthew's or Justin's birth times could have made their birthdays be apart by three days? Two hours later for Matthew's entrance into the world would make his birthday July 1st and two hours earlier for Justin would make his birthday June 29th. It wasn't meant to be, and the kids had a bond as close as their birthdays.

This is not quite the end of the story. Matthew's birthday party was to be held later on that day at a local amusement park. At about 4 a.m., when things finally quieted down, the nurses took the baby, I kissed Sue goodnight, and I left for home to grab some sleep and prepare for the party. I have to tell you, when I arrived at the park and all of the other mothers heard about our happy *new* news, they just took over completely. They made sure all the kids got on rides, had enough pizza to eat, juice to drink, and that all had a splendid time. It was the easiest birthday party I *didn't* run! But the hardest thing to do still remained. I needed to make sure that Matthew understood how special he was and how special it was to have a baby brother. I pulled him over to the side at some point during the party. I pointed over to all of the colorful presents standing in the corner. I told him that those presents were great, but his best present was in the hospital with mommy. For whatever reason, he bought it, and Matthew and Justin to this day are the best of buds. They love each other immensely and that bond will never be broken.

Interestingly, as close as they are to one another, that's how different they are in their approach to living their lives. Justin runs his life slow and steady. You know what they say about that. He wins the race every time. Matthew is more intense, yet the results are the same. Whereas Matthew will finish an assignment before it was even handed out, Justin will finish it the morning it is due. This would drive Sue and me bonkers, but to his credit, Justin never gave us the chance to admonish him over his laid-back technique. He ended up 8th in the senior class, graduated with high honors, and is presently attending Brown University. Go figure. Two kids from the same loins, yet light years apart in their approach to things. Vive la difference!

Shandi

Before Matthew and Justin arrived on the scene, there was Shandi. Projecting the image of the "All-American" couple, Sue and I did things in fitting order…got married, bought a house, and of course got a dog. Sue's oldest sister and her husband owned a beautiful Siberian husky with wolf-like facial features and two different colored eyes, common for that breed of dog. They hooked up their female husky, Shasha, with a male version of the same breed and suddenly, there was a large litter of pups. They were able to sell the new arrivals seeing that they all had the "Good Housekeeping" seal of approval from the American Kennel Club. But the smallest puppy, and probably the cutest, was ear marked for a special place…our lovely new home! Great house warming gift, huh? Truth be told, Sue and I were asked if we wanted to take on the responsibility of owning a dog…the runt wasn't just left on our doorstep. Now, Sue was a cat owner back in her younger, pre-married days, and I never had a large pet at all (other than a parakeet). In retrospect, owning a new house was a full time job in itself, so probably, Sue and I should have reneged on the offer. We couldn't say no after viewing the alluring eyes and face of the puppy.

Next in line…a name for the doggie. Sue's parents and younger sister had travelled to England one summer and one story that stuck with us was the unusual food and drink they encountered across the "pond." England is not renowned for its quaff, but Sue's folks did mention a drink that they tried and actually enjoyed. It was a seemingly strange mixture of beer and lemonade, and it was called a "shandy". Sue and I liked that name, and even though we never imbibed one, we called our runt, our one and only child at the time, Shandi.

Now the house was new for us, and Sue and I decided that Shandi, a Siberian Husky, a breed of dog used to the outdoor elements, would be much more comfortable utilizing our backyard as her permanent residence and playpen. I went to the local hardware store and purchased a whole mess of stuff so I could build a fenced in pen for Shandi to sleep in overnight. We were aware that Shandi would grow, so I made the dimensions extra large thinking ahead for the future. All the while that I was toiling away outside nailing two-by-fours together, securing a plywood floor, and finally constructing a chain link fence around its perimeter, Shandi was intently watching me through the patio door from inside the house. She had a kind of sly look on her face, almost an expression of confusion. "What is that?" and "Who's that for?" "Certainly, not me!" At the time, I guess Sue and I weren't very good at interpreting doggie expressions, so I continued on and finished the luxurious "penthouse" (running water, eat-in kitchen, etc) for the queen.

It was now time to introduce Shandi to her new abode. With much struggle, Sue and I coaxed her in by tossing a cooked hamburger in the enclosure. Day turned into night, and Sue and I went out to wish Shandi a peaceful night's rest. We turned away from her, heading back into the house, and the howling started. I'm not talking about the Brandner horror novel, but Shandi's howling was a horror. It was constant, loud and piercing...all night long! Sue and I figured that if we went out there and gave in to Shandi's calls, we would never train her to be an outside dog, a trait of that breed. Was she being obstinate or dumb? Come on, you're a Siberian Husky. You were supposed to love the outside and all of its imposing features. Make your relatives proud of you. After all, they were pulling sleds in tall banks of snow, braving the cold gusts of wind, the freezing temperatures. You know, you could be out there heading an Iditarod team. There were a lot of reasons for Shandi to see it our way, but apparently, none seemed to cross her mind. She was like a horse with blinders. One direction, one train of thought—get me out of here! The yelping continued for about a week, and Sue and I were starting to melt. Many nights, we looked at each other in utter frustration and said, "You go this time. Get her and bring her in." We were always on the precipice of succumbing, but we held back. It was very tough to hear her night after night, and it seemed that she was winning the war of wills.

It all came to a head on the sixth day of our attempt to familiarize her with our backyard surroundings. Sue and I were eating dinner when a knock on the front door sounded. Who could it be? My first thought was that it was a neighbor coming to bring us the proverbial "cup of sugar" welcoming us into their friendly town. I opened the door to reveal a policeman standing outside. He wasn't holding any cups of sugar, but instead he palmed a pad with lots of scribble on it. "Do you own a dog?" "Why, yes, we do." "One of your neighbors is complaining that she barks all night long and it's disturbing to hear. You must either get rid of it or make some other arrangements." I retorted, "Well, thanks for the warm welcome into the neighborhood, officer! Don't you worry; we'll take care of it." We took care of the problem all right. From that night on, Shandi had a new home to live in…ours! In my eyes, she was a disgrace to her fellow Huskies. Shandi made herself *very* comfortable in our house and quickly became an indoor fixture. Her face may have resembled a wolf, but she was sly like a fox and she won the war and got her way in the end. I dismantled the pen and scrapped all of my work. Look at the bright side, Sue and I did get our total backyard back, and yes, we were allowed to stay on the block!

Sue and I really didn't have it in us to ignore Shandi's cries, so all parties were satisfied. By the way, little did we know but this Shandi scream epic set the standard for how Sue and I were to deal with Matthew and Justin. Matthew was an infant that never wanted to be laid down so putting him to sleep at night was a real trip. Many nights, Sue placed him in our bed just so when he started crying, she didn't have far to go to feed him. I remember that Matthew's lack of giving her downtime nearly put Sue in the loony bin. I recall her screaming out loud at the ceiling, angry at her mother for leaving us too early in life, and why wasn't she here to help. Unfortunately, Sue's mom as previously mentioned in an earlier chapter, had died of breast cancer three months before Matthew's birth. Everything was caving in on Sue, emotionally and physically. She really had no aid whatsoever. Sue didn't really feel comfortable asking my mom, and many of our friends were married, but still childless, so they too, had no experience at child rearing. I was working at my teaching job and Sue was on maternity leave from school so the onus kind of fell on her to see to Matthew's incessant needs. But she was tired, and needed her rest as well, but Matthew needed 24/7 attention. It got to the unbearable point one evening that I instructed Sue to go into our bedroom, lock the door and leave Matthew with me. Sue required that peace and quiet period so badly. I got firsthand what Sue was experiencing every night. I literally walked and paced around the coffee table in the living room all night long holding Matthew in my arms or near my chest. Matthew just wouldn't go to sleep. I remember placing him in a mechanical swing which kept him moving for a half hour. But as soon as the mechanism stopped, Matthew started crying; he was uncanny. I held him all night and of course I was a wreck the next day at school. But it needed to be done for everyone's sake.

Sue and I pow-wowed and obviously we knew that we needed to do something. This was the night. The plan was to put Matthew down in his crib and if necessary, let him cry it out until he tired himself out to sleep. As painful as this was going to be, there was no alternative at this point. We bunker down and huddle together in our bed unable to drown out Matthew's cry, but we also knew that this was so necessary to do. We both thought of our Shandi episode, but unlike that fiasco, the shrieks were not heard by any neighbors, just us. Many times we had to hold each other back from getting up out of bed to go hold and comfort our baby. Sound like our Shandi escapade? Thirty-two minutes later…yes, I timed it…the crying stopped. We got up to peer into his room, and Matthew was literally sleeping like a baby. We needed to do this routine a couple more evenings, but the crying diminished each succeeding night and eventually ceased completely. Mission accomplished. Not that I'm comparing Matthew to Shandi, but they were both our babies, and we never wanted to hurt them in any way. Sue and I for the most part, were mushes when it came to dealing with our kids…Shandi, Matthew and Justin! By the way, I didn't mention Justin in this, partly because he is the second child and they never get any attention (I can relate with that!), but mainly because he was not a troublesome sleeper. He made it much easier on us and if and when a problem did occur, Sue and I used what we learned from our Shandi and Matthew episode and became pros at the baby-rearing game!

Back to Shandi…Sue and I now basically found ourselves in a strange situation. Shandi, a "pack" animal supposedly used to the outdoor wilds, found herself indoors instead in a tame, civilized environment of a cozy home. What to do, what to do? We had some work to do. Sue and I knew that we couldn't change the house to suit her, so our goal was clear…transform Shandi into a "cultured" beast! She needed to be housebroken before she broke the house. The way we spoiled her, she was already eating table scraps from our fine china, and sitting comfortably on our favorite lounge chair in the living room. We never could master Shandi's ability to use a fork and knife, but she loved reading the _New York Times_! You can see clearly which one of the three of us ran the show. But, Sue and I needed to put our paw, I mean foot down about certain things like letting us know when it was bathroom time. She trained us pretty well on that account, but we also needed to be able to leave the house for a length of time and find it in one piece when we returned before she resorted back to being an animal! Our approach came from a book Sue found in the library dealing with dog discipline. The idea seemed to make sense to us, but we wondered if it made sense to Shandi. The thought process is for your dog to gain trust in you. So Sue and I obeyed the book. We left her in the house alone with some of her favorite toys for five minutes. We did so, and when we got back, Shandi greeted us with wild enthusiasm. See Shandi, mommy and daddy came back…we weren't going to leave you forever. Each time we did this, we extended the span of time…ten, fifteen, twenty, and then twenty-five minutes. Everything was going great. Not a single piece of furniture or lamp or table disrupted. Each time, however, Shandi's response to our reentering the house was more animated, more frantic. We figured it was her way of saying hello, welcome back, and nice to see ya again.

Okay, we now go for the big one…time to push the envelope to half an hour! We go out and enjoy a cup of coffee together at a local bistro. We were having a grand old time alone, out for an "evening" and not worrying too much about Shandi. We checked our watches. It was time to head home and greet and praise our baby for being a good girl. Sue and I arrived home very confidently, only to see clumps of foam rubber flying through the air, almost as if two people had a pillow fight with the feathers dancing in the wind currents. That favorite chair I mentioned earlier was no more. We were now able to notice the fine craftsmanship of the inner parts of the chair, the heavy duty springs and the thickness of the fabric used to upholster the lounge seat! Well done Shandi. I guess it was another example of how Sue and I misread our "child." Her agitated, tumultuous reaction to our coming back after twenty-five minutes was a prelude to her eating the sofa. Now I'm not suggesting that Shandi was able to tell time, but I could tell you this…we never left her alone in the living sections of the house for more than twenty-five minutes at a clip! I calculated that if one year of our lives is equivalent to seven dog years, then a half an hour of human time to a dog translates to a load of doggie hours...no wonder Shandi went ballistic on the chair.

Sue, Shandi, and I eventually came to an understanding about the "rules" of the house, not without its trials and tribulations. We pretty much agreed to all of Shandi's demands and then and only then was all right with the world! Now there were weekends when Sue and I needed a vacation from the routine of everyday life. Our love at the time was to go camping in designated grounds. We were not the "Daniel Boone" types. Sue and I enjoyed the outdoors, but with certain amenities...a spigot with running water, a flat campsite free of rocks and twigs, a porta-john relatively nearby the site and beautiful weather. When we first started camping, we would pack minimally, maybe a tent and two sleeping bags that could be zipped together. We evolved into high-end campers as the years passed including such items as air mattresses with cigarette lighter plug-in pumps to electrically blow them up, propane stoves and lanterns, screen tent, bug zappers to list just a few comforts. There was a time when Sue and I decided after we settled into a campsite that we had set up with all of the aforementioned equipment to move everything to a different spot. The water spigot was too far down the path! Unfortunately we noticed this "catastrophe" a bit too late so the tents came down, the poles packed back into the car, and the air mattresses next. You see it took at least an hour of loud, ticking motor-pumping sound to get these inflated to our satisfaction (we weren't too popular with our friendly campers adjacent to us because of it!) so Sue and I weren't about to let the air out. Our Toyota Corolla, a tiny car, already filled to the brim with other the camping supplies also needed to house a puffed-up cushion. Here Sue and I are, pushing, cramming, and struggling to do the impossible. After a while, we threw our hands up in the air, and I ended up driving the vehicle with the back door open, with half an air mattress protruding out of the side of the car! Luckily, we were transplanting ourselves just down the dirt road to a nicer site…was it worth it? We thought so at the time. Sure, we didn't mind the laughter from the other campers as we drove by with our bulging cargo! We had never taken part in those college pranks seeing how many people could fit into a phone booth, or how many could pile into a Volkswagen but Sue and I got the idea that day.

It was events like that one that made Sue and I actually smarten up to the point where camping eventually meant make reservations at a nice hotel! But in our earlier, "young and foolish" years we braved the elements and faced Mother Nature head-on. The one "item" we couldn't bring along with us unfortunately, was a pet. We needed to leave Shandi in capable hands, with people that knew how to deal with animals, comfortable having fur flying throughout their household…my parents. This was asking the captain of the Titanic to watch out for icebergs! My folks, bless them, never had an animal. The only things that came close to being animalistic in their lives were me and my brother! So this was going to be an adventurous weekend at best.

Getting Shandi in the car to take her to Shirley, a town in Suffolk County on Long Island was a trip in itself. Nervously jumping from front seat to back seat and visa versa, she knew something was happening. We packed all of her play toys and tons of food even though Sue and I knew that mom was going to be feeding her delicious homemade Italian meatballs, lasagna, and cannolis. I really wanted to switch roles with Shandi realizing the royal treatment that was to follow. Sue and I dropped her off and grudgingly left her behind. Remember, this was our baby.

Sue and I made it to upstate New York to our favorite campsite without a single phone call to my parents. No cell phones in those days, but the campgrounds had lots of pay phones, so it seemed like every hour on the hour (we brought a boat load of quarters just for this), one of us annoyingly called to check in on Shandi's progress. During the second day of our camping excursion, Sue talked to mom and she was told that everything was fine. Little did we know that trouble had brewed right there in Shirley. Sue and I became aware of this incident years later, but we were kept in the dark not to scare us. One of my parent's neighbors came by to visit mom and dad (it must have been the alluring smell of Italian food), and accidently left the garage door ajar. Well, that's all the room Shandi needed to bolt from the house. She was a pack animal probably looking for some sled to pull! Dad saw that she was nowhere to be seen so he went into action. Smartly, he grabbed a meatball from the stove and took off after Shandi. The Long Island Railroad tracks just happen to be a couple blocks on ground level from my folks' home. To this day, I don't know why dad headed in that direction, but we were glad he did. He found her. There was Shandi, parked directly on the train rails, a diesel's headlight rapidly approaching, and dad running, huffing, and puffing trying desperately to reach her before the train did, waving his arms, a stick in his left hand to flag down the oncoming train, and a meatball in his right hand hoping Shandi would be tempted by its odor. What a scene that must have been. Panic set in on the parts of Shandi and dad, not the motorman. For whatever reason, maybe the vibrations on the metal tracks caused by the humongous train, or maybe the attractive aroma of mom's meatball, Shandi decided to vacate the premises. The train came flying by at rapid speed (funny, that never seems to occur when you're sitting on the train!) and probably distracted Shandi just enough so that dad could collar her. Episode over, but boy, it must have been hair-raising. I guess you can teach old dogs new tricks...I'm referring to my parents. Being scared of a repeat performance, they locked every door in the house and didn't leave their home for the rest of the weekend.

It was four years into our life with Shandi when Matthew was born. Shandi was pretty shrewd and probably realized that change was in the air. She noticed that Sue and I were doing something different spending less time with her and instead preparing a bedroom for a new arrival, plastering new wall paper, gluing a rainbow border paper near the ceiling, painting a wall-sized rainbow to match the new border wallpaper that we had put up, and laying down a new rug (just as it stands today, except the room is now our Command Central...computer, phone, fax). Yes, the baby's room was complete and it was off-limits to Shandi. After four years of having the run of the house, and pretty much running our lives, Shandi became very territorial. Siberian Huskies are in general. So Sue and I were a bit leery of what she might do knowing there was a new inhabitant in the household. Just about this time even though Sue and I took great care of her, Shandi developed a case of fleas and wouldn't you know it, when Shandi wasn't available, the fleas used Sue as the host. As I mentioned before, Matthew was not an easy baby, so combine that fact with the fear of Shandi "exploring" Matthew and now a flea infestation as well, it was time for Sue and me to pow-wow again. The convincing incident that told us Shandi's days were numbered happened when one day, she nosed her way into the baby's room, stood on her hind legs leaning against the side of the wooden crib, and peered down at Matthew. Now we don't think that she would have done any harm to him, but you only get one chance in life and we didn't want to tempt fate. To be fair, we held a family vote, Sue, me, and Shandi, to see whether or not she should go...the result was two to one in favor of her departure. I'm not at liberty to divulge the actual votes by any of the individuals but let's just say that voter turn-out was heavy. It was not easy to let go of a member of the family and Shandi was all of that.

Sue and I put ads in the papers hopeful that we would

find a happy new home for her. After all, she was a good dog, friend, and companion, and she deserved nothing less. A lady who lived out in Holbrook, a town between Oceanside and Shirley, answered the ad and Sue and I took a ride to see if this was to be suitable. She had a big, beautiful, fenced in backyard, exactly what a pack animal required, as well as two kids, one ten years old and another eight. It certainly looked like a loving environment (do you think we should have given it a second thought when we noticed the numerous stuffed animal heads mounted on the walls of her den?), and it turned out to be perfect for Shandi. We never went back to visit Shandi for fear that we'd start crying again, just like the day we said good-bye to her. By the way, the next year on Father's Day, the new owner called us and asked if we wanted to come to her home for a barbeque. Why Father's Day you may ask? She knew that in our hearts there would always be a place for Sue's and my first child, Shandi!

Nine Months of Chemotherapy

After Sue's cancer diagnosis in 1992, it was time to start an aggressive protocol to combat the disease. Sue was young enough (40 years old) and her body was strong enough to handle the rigors of chemotherapy. After consulting two oncologists, it was decided that the best approach would be an aggressive nine-month bombardment of drugs. The first three-month regimen of Adriamycin knocked Sue out. She was tired, slightly nauseous, and she lost her hair completely. If knowing the fact that Sue now had to deal with cancer wasn't enough, the reality of losing her hair was devastating and nearly put us over the top. It was traumatic to see her hair, once so silky brown and beautiful, falling out, root and all, with every brush and comb stroke.

The next six months had Sue on a regimen of three rounds of chemo, a concoction of Cytoxan, Methotrexate, and 5FU (no, I didn't make that name up). These drugs were not as bad for Sue to tolerate, and despite the fact that she dreaded having to be subjected to this, she was a real trooper. We needed to access her veins every three weeks to inject the chemotherapy. We were scared, depressed, angry, and unsure where all of this was headed. The unknown can be a frightful event, especially when the unknown involves cancer! The day after every treatment was "Flowers Day". I would buy Sue a bouquet of freshly cut flowers from a local florist hoping that it would brighten her day a bit. My role had changed from husband to husband/caregiver. I tried my best to make Sue as comfortable as possible. My attitude towards everyday things changed as well. Suddenly, all the little things that could wedge in between a solid married couple were no longer important to deal with. It didn't matter if the garbage wasn't taken out for a few days or if the dishes lay in the sink for a week—it just didn't matter. I still feel this way today. My perception of life has been completely altered by Sue's illness, and for the better, I believe. Little things just don't bother me any more. Our focus was to see Sue coping as well as she could with the side effects of the chemo. If it was possible, Sue became even more important to me than ever before—probably to a fault. I felt it was my job to constantly hold the net under Sue so I could be there if and when she fell. She would actually get angry with me for doting over her too much. I sometimes wanted to do everything for her, and instead I was probably smothering her. I didn't realize that it was okay if she had the drive and energy to do something, to let her do it. I didn't realize that it was okay to make her feel "whole" and live as normal a life as possible. Instead my overbearingness probably made her feel more like a cancer patient. I was wrong, but at the time, I was doing what I thought was the correct thing to do.

Sue's reaction to my hovering caused me to walk on eggshells, fearful that my actions of caring and love would be misconstrued. The one thing I certainly didn't want to happen was for Sue to get angry with me for what I thought was loving consideration for her. I would have to learn to be there for her when *she* wanted me there, not when *I* thought it was necessary.

This was a brand new situation in our lives and it took us some time to learn how to deal with it and each other. Think of Sue and me being in two different boats trying to get into a third boat together. The boat would rock a bit initially as we stepped into it, but eventually it would stop wavering and rocking and it would settle down. It's at that point in time that you can now guide the boat and take control of the situation. This is what both Sue and I faced—a brand new phase of our life together and we eventually got it right.

During this nine-month period, Sue and I were so focused and concerned about her getting better that I hate to admit it, but our kids took a back seat. Mind you, they were in school for much of that time, and school tended to take up much of their focus. We were blessed to have kids who cared about their education. Sue started the chemo in November, 1992 and ended it in the summertime month of July, 1993. We tried to do things with the kids, but the cancer's side effects did hamper our ability to go all out with them. Being tired and nauseous, Sue really didn't want to be too far away from home. We did do the normal trips to Grandma and Grandpa's home for Thanksgiving, Christmas, New Year's, and Easter, but these too were a burden on Sue. Many times, she would excuse herself to sleep on their living room couch or bedroom bed. Everyone understood and was always respectful of Sue's needs.

That first Christmas of 1992 was particularly difficult to navigate. We both knew that we had to make it "normal" for our kids, but it was hard to do. Putting up the tree with all of its sentimental ornaments—our first year married, Matt and Justin's first Christmases, decorations that Sue and I had picked up from our trips—all served as reminders of our very cloudy journey ahead. Would this be the last Christmas that we would be all together? Would this be the last time we'd be sending out a holiday picture card with the four of us in it?

We did get through the holiday season with our best, forced smiles and the kids seemed to enjoy their gifts. One great present that Sue and I got for the boys was a little known video game named LOLO. It was not your typical "shoot-um up" violent game that was very popular at the time, instead it was a thinking man's game. Mazes and traps and well-placed enemies who had certain powers set all over the board made for wonderful family fun as we all sat around the television shouting out suggestions as to how to navigate through the perilous journey. It got a bit heated when Sue and I would ask Matthew to try a particular move or path, and Matthew was already miles ahead seeing why that wouldn't work. Justin, only four years old, was not dexterous enough yet to handle some of the fast moves that needed to be accomplished to get through a level. Only Matthew had "LOLO" hands so he was always our DC, or designated controller. Justin did his share of helping us through the boards. I remember the morning after Christmas, Justin and Matthew came into our bedroom and wanted us to join them downstairs in the den to play the video game. This followed a long evening of playing the game that left us at Level Two. The kids were anxiously into the game, and even though Sue was so tired from her chemo (it was earlier in the week that she had the treatment), she was a trooper. Everything for the kids...normality was the name of the game...show the kids that you're all right. And that's exactly what we did. We set up a blanket on the den couch, she laid down on it, we all covered her with part of it, and the four of us were in business. She, even in her "chemo" condition, came up with the one path that led us to victory on that first board of LOLO that morning. As you successfully got through one level, the subsequent levels were harder to deal with...sound familiar...that was to be Sue's and my life living with cancer! LOLO was great fun for all of us. The company that made the game (HAL) eventually went out of business after producing LOLO 2 and LOLO 3. I could definitely figure out why. This was a different sort of video game. Not much glitz, pomp and circumstance, just good clean delightfully lovable characters in a thought-provoking setting. Try to get your hands on the game...you thinkers will like it!

♋♋♋

That first kiss between Sue and me ushering in the New Year 1993 was particularly long and loving. Neither of us wanted to let go, knowing the prospect of a new year with our challenges was leading us down that—to quote the Beatles—"Long and Winding Road" with hope and tons of trepidation.

As the chemo treatments continued, we started to see the developing patterns of side effects. Three days after the infusion, Sue was totally out of commission. She was tired, listless, dispirited, and barely wanting to eat, talk, or even listen to television or radio. Chemo has this nasty habit of building up in your body, and each impending treatment could intensify the side effects after the next one. Sue was fairly fortunate that that didn't happen, but we were constantly waiting for the other shoe to drop. We never took anything for granted and remained vigilant during the and days and weeks after the chemotherapy.

Seeing that Sue's post chemo weeks were somewhat bearable after the first few days, we decided to do something to brighten the family's spirits and have a change of pace. Having been through the first six months of treatments with relatively few side effects, we decided it was time to start living again. We talked about driving down to Florida where Sue's youngest sister, Terri, lived. She stayed in a beautiful complex where there was access to paddleball courts, golf courses, a swimming pool, and a scenic walkway around the complex. Terri, being a good cook and wonderful host, assured us that Sue would not have to lift a finger and could just lay out enjoying all the comforts that Florida had to offer. Our job was to run this idea past our oncologist, and assuming he thought it was okay, to start packing. He not only thought it would be a good idea, but he gave us his blessings. We worked out the treatment day so that our trip would be after Sue's post chemo "reaction" week and we were hoping for calm and normalcy the next week. The oncologist was very savvy as well as caring. He gave us the phone number of an oncologist friend of his in the area we were to visit just in case of any unforeseen events. His enthusiasm gave us the impetus to take on this venture. We had never driven such far distances, especially with a nine and four-year-old in the van. Not only was it important to us to show our kids that they were not forgotten in this tumult called cancer but we still could have fun as a family unit. It was important to Sue and me to prove to ourselves that we were facing the beast, and we were determined not to let it beat us or slow us down.

Our packing had to be altered just a bit due to Sue's situation. We bought lots of sunscreen lotion, and two beautiful wide-brimmed sun hats for Sue to wear while lounging around the pool. Sunrays and chemo do not mix well, so we took all precautions to assure Sue's safety. No two-piece bathing suits for Sue as well. We didn't need overexposure. To show my support, I too wore a one-piece suit! I packed the van with all the luggage, lots of VHS movies for the kids to watch (we had a portable television/VHS player with a cigarette lighter power supply cord) and waited for the end of school before Easter break. Sue and I never pulled the kids out of school for anything so at 3:05 p.m. on Friday, with the car totally packed, we picked up Matt and Justin from school and off we went. That was my last teaching day as well at Parkland High School, so we had a hopefully glorious week ahead of us. Our plan was to drive to North Carolina by midnight. We booked a hotel right off of I-95 so we could bed down, refresh overnight, then finish the rest of the grueling trek to Florida.

The kids and Sue sat in the back seats of the van while I drove. The hottest video for Matt and Justin at the time was Disney's *The Brave Little Toaster*. They could watch it over and over again. Funny thing, to this day, I have yet to see the video, but I could recite all of the lines by heart recognizing any character by its voice! You would be able to do the same after hearing it in its entirety at least five times on the way to Carolina. Driving has its disadvantages!

When Matt wasn't watching the video, he occupied his time by journaling. He brought a little book with him for the car ride so he could document such vital events as the time, the place, the moment that we stopped at gas stations, bathroom rest stops, and McDonald's to "fuel" up. The first day/evening of the trip was thankfully uneventful. We got to North Carolina a little after midnight and our glorious one room, two-bed shack was waiting for us. Our heads collectively hit the pillows, and we were in dreamland instantly. That night, I remember envisioning the Brave Little Toaster saving his friend Appliance, the lamp!

We woke up early to get a nice start on the next and final part of the journey. As a family, we were singing songs, playing car trip games like identifying as many different state license plates as we could, and in general, having a great family experience. I forgot about cancer, chemo, and side effects and instead had a wonderful time with my family.

I know we were somewhere in Florida on I-95 in the fast lane. At this point in the trek, it was just a matter of getting there at all costs. We had been on the road most of the day and we all were tired. I stepped on the gas pedal to get us there even faster, but I noticed that the van wasn't responding to the request for more speed. As a matter of fact, the van was doing the exact opposite, slowing down instead. I barely was able to amble over two lanes to the right hand shoulder coming to a complete stop. Now I was terrified and frustrated. I looked at the gas gauge, which was reading full. Sue remembered Matt's journal, and knowing Matt, we knew his records would be impeccable. I asked him to check on the last gas-up we had. Matt flipped through his pages and said, "Two states ago!" I guess when you're driving long distances, having a good time with your family, things like fill-ups take (excuse the expression) a back seat. I also wasn't concentrating on highway signs, so I had no idea how far the next or last exit was to our position. We had no cell phones at the time, so I had a major decision to make as dusk approached—do I leave my family in the van on the side of I-95 and pick a direction and start walking, or do we stick together as a unit and cry together? We voted on staying together, so Sue and

I began frantically waving any thing we could in the air to flag someone down to help us. About a half an hour passed (including some State Troopers, may I add) and nary a soul stopped for us. We began to lose faith, and lose our minds, but finally, a car pulled over behind us. It was a beaten up old Chevy driven by a man who seemed to be on a mission. I gave him the membership number on my AAA card and asked if he wouldn't mind going to the next exit and calling it in at a pay phone. He peered into the van and noticed Matt and Justin, worn and frazzled from the events of the day. He obliged and sped off. We all huddled back in the van waiting patiently for an AAA tow truck to come along. About fifteen minutes elapsed, and who pulled up behind but that beaten up old Chevy once again. It was that man on that mission. He had with him a plastic gas tank filled with five gallons of fuel, and waters and sodas for the kids. He said that he just finished his term of duty in the army, and he was heading home from Washington State to Miami where he lived. He said he had stopped to help at least twenty people stranded like us along his travels home. He wouldn't tell me his name nor take any money for his troubles. He wished us a safe rest of the trip and with that, he sped off again. Wow…Sue and I thought that angels do exist right here on earth. Other than the "angel" nurses who worked in the oncology office, we hadn't experienced something like that. We were both grateful and dumbfounded at the same moment. Maybe we were blessed or lucky enough in meeting this gentleman and maybe we could carry over the same feeling when it came to Sue's health situation. Maybe we would be blessed or lucky enough to beat this cancer.

So, our trip continued on without a hitch (or a hitch needed!). I obsessively made sure to fill up the van every two hours on the nose, seeing that the gas gauge was faulty. We arrived at Terri's home a little later than expected, but there nonetheless. The week was filled with good times, good food at the Seder for Passover, good rest lying by the pool, and good talk. After all, this was the first time the sisters had seen each other since the diagnosis back in September. It was very emotional at times, but a beautiful thing to witness Sue living with cancer and living normally, actually appearing to be enjoying life, smiling, laughing and quipping as the "old" Sue used to act.

As they say, all good things must end. Somewhere on the way back to Long Island, I guess the reality of the situation struck me. We were headed back to our home, our routine, to a life filled with chemo, side effects, and uncertainty. The only certainty was that Sue still had three months of chemotherapy treatments to finish. But somewhere in the recesses of our minds, Sue and I simultaneously were filled with hope and promise that we could and would beat this disease.

The remaining months of treatment came and went with similar side effect reactions as before. Sue began to gain her strength back as we approached the final infusion. As Sue's strength was rejuvenated, she felt more and more comfortable both mentally and physically and she was now able to volunteer in the local PTA. Since she was a pro at the computer, she began producing some of the prettiest school newsletters that Oceanside ever saw. Sue also gave of her time aiding teachers during school functions and trips, and in general she was becoming "Sue" once again. She also, started to gain back her hair. It was peach fuzzy at first, and then continued to grow in curly, totally different from her long straight hair, pre-chemo. That alone gave us encouragement and affirmation that we had been to hell and back, looking towards the future confidently, yet vigilantly.

Music in Our Lives

Music is all around us and does become an integral part of our lives, even if it only serves as a reminder of where you were in time when a particular tune is played on the radio. You don't have to be "musical" to find yourself tapping your toes or lip-syncing to your favorite song. For me, it was recreational, seeing that I have zero musical talent. I did pretend to sing like Paul McCartney of the Beatles, though unfortunately I didn't have his ability, his looks, or his British accent (I did play lefty *air guitar*). Three strikes—I'm out! For Sue, it was in her; a huge, beautiful part of her life.

Sue was always a classy lady, so classy that she played classical piano from childhood. Sue told me about her piano teacher and described him as an old school kind of guy. He was a taskmaster; strict, stayed to the book, and expected miracles, at times from his students. Sue tried hard to meet his expectations. I think she not only met his expectations, she superseded them! I'm not just saying this because it was Sue, but I think she played beautifully. She would be the first to tell you that she wasn't any good at it. But this was Sue, never bragging about her accomplishments, rather putting herself down. She was so humble and truly never wanted the spotlight on her. My musicality ended the day I was told that I couldn't play the drums in the projects we lived in when I was a kid. I later found out this rule was enforced only on me—probably the powers that be heard how poorly I played. The projects had paper-thin walls, and drumming would have driven my neighbors up a paper-thin wall! So my desire to play any form of music was snuffed out at the tender age of ten. I'm glad Sue, as a child, lived in an apartment where piano playing was acceptable and the walls were thicker.

I would love sitting in the den and listening to Sue play Mozart, Bach, Beethoven, and Debussy. I would love to sing, even though I really couldn't. Before I sang with Sue at the keyboard, we would tape up all of the windows in the house to protect them from my harsh voice waves; this was neither live, nor Memorex! Sue would play Beatles tunes and other pop rock oldies from the 60s and 70s. She had that knack of being able to look at a "fake" book of music and play from it.

It was because of Sue's influence that Matthew and Justin took classical piano lessons. Their piano teacher, a wonderful lady, became more than just a teacher. She became a great friend as well, and to top off the many connections, she too shared the same birthday as our kids, June 30th. Sue knew how important it was to have music in her own life, and she wanted the kids to experience that grand feeling as well. Both Matthew and Justin, being mathematicians, took to playing the piano quite easily. There is a definite tie between music and math. They played so well at their concerts. Sue and I would wait with nervous anticipation in the audience as their turn to play arose. Inevitably they would play without a hitch, and I would cry with pride. At times, Sue would play a duet with the kids as well. I thought of how beautiful they sounded, and I hoped that they would play together forever.

I mentioned earlier that Sue worked in a very low-income area in a high school in Brooklyn. The kids in this area were deprived of many of the good things that life could offer simply because of their surroundings and environment. Sue, a math teacher, did her very best to make the kids feel important and proud of whom they are. Sue befriended a wonderful music teacher in the school, and together, the Cantique was born. This was to be an annual event in the school where kids would learn how to play an instrument, usually piano, and perform in front of their peers. Mind you, this school didn't have great facilities. The kids would actually practice on homemade crayon cardboard piano keyboards. Sue, as well as other very dedicated teachers, would help the piano teacher in any way they could to expose these kids to some culture. The end result was an incredible experience for not only the performing students, but for the performing teachers of the school as well. Every year, Sue performed a classical piece on the piano. She was always nervous playing in front of a crowd, but she rose to the occasion. This Cantique idea grew over the years. The music teacher, Sue, and I would host it at our respective homes. The students, and in later years, the former graduate students would come back to play and participate along with many teachers from school. Even the kids of the teachers, now in their teens, would perform as well. One year, Sue and Justin played the piano, Matthew played the guitar, and I stood in front of a map of the United States. They played the "States Song" made famous by a cartoon called *The Animaniacs*, while I tried desperately to point out all of the states. The song gets pretty fast, so it becomes funny to try to keep up with the music. In other years, the kids and Sue would play classical pieces from their repertoire. All in all, it was a great experience for everyone, and I was always bursting with tears of joy over how Matthew, Justin, and Sue performed. No matter how badly Sue was weakened by the side effects of her chemo treatments, she always prepared diligently for many months prior to the Cantique. It actually gave her a goal, a purpose, and certainly, a distraction from the daily thoughts pervading her mind about cancer. The Cantique was a wonderful concept, and the kids and adults got a chance to expand their horizons because of it. Sue was always very proud to be a part of the annual Cantiques.

One of our great joys was when we celebrated our 25th wedding anniversary. Sue and I took music to an all time low that evening. We rented a boat, a Mississippi Steamer with paddle wheel and all for a three-hour cruise (sound familiar?). We also celebrated Matthew graduating high school as valedictorian and his acceptance to Princeton University, as well as Justin's 13th birthday. The boat was supplied with good food, drinks, and all of our family, friends, and colleagues from school. It was just like our wedding except this time, the dance floor was floating. The boat traveled through the inlets of Long Island. It was a beautiful night, and everyone seemingly had a good time. The best was yet to come, however. You see, Sue and I had prepared a little candle lighting ceremony. We honored our wonderful guests and family for all of their support through Sue's ordeal with cancer, and we spoke of our two great kids, Matthew and Justin. At the end of each speech, Sue and I lit a candle. Now came the coup-de-grâce. We wanted to honor ourselves, and our beautiful marriage of twenty-five years. We didn't just read a speech for us, but instead had a little surprise for the unsuspecting guests. We called up to the dais, our brother-in-law, who just so happened to play the fiddle. While he was on his way up, Sue and I changed into new clothing. I came out dressed in rags, a ratty cap and moldy beard emulating a Jewish Russian peasant while Sue, playing my wife, donned a shawl, a kerchief over her head and a torn sweater. Our brother-in-law was in on the gag as Sue and I began to sing a song from a popular 1960's Broadway play set in tsarist Russia, but with a slight twist. We sang our sentiments to naturally fit our twenty-five years of marriage. As our brother-in-law began to fiddle, I melodically asked Sue if she adored me. The fun began with Sue's and my responses to each other. Some of the highlights, or should I say "lowlights", included Sue singing about how I gained weight during the past twenty-five years quipping that she had watched me grow from side to side instead of head to toe! I retort indicating that throughout all of the years, she endured my jokes, my puns…which were no fun! We continued by musically stating that when Sue met me in Brooklyn College, she was swooning, I was failing and we both fell on our calcul-asses! We concluded by singing our love and acceptance for each other after all those years of marriage making this an event to remember.

Sue and I gave each other a hug and big kiss, and the throng gave us a standing ovation after we were done. It was a touching song with a comedic flavor and was appreciated by our guests. I truly believe that many in the crowd admired Sue for how she was conducting herself while battling this dreaded disease, and part of that applause was for her and her courage. It was true. Sue never showed people outwardly any fear or dismay. While in public, she never felt sorry for herself, and instead, tried to live every day to its fullest. So many friends would tell her how she was a role model for how they wanted to live their lives.

Just to be sure that no one would leave the boat during our bad rendition of the song, I had all lifeboats detached from the Steamer before we left port. I think it was reported later that only two guests jumped overboard when I started to sing (only kidding)! Sue was a trouper because she was so shy, but went along with the gag to please me. I think she was happy she did it afterwards. Yes, we took music a step backwards with that performance, but at least it was memorable.

♋♋♋

As it turned out, Sue and I shared a love for classical singers from the early 1930's and 40's. So our first ever movie (that we actually attended and watched!) was *Lady Sings the Blues* with Diana Ross playing the part of Billie Holliday. It had great music along with a very sad story of how Ms. Holliday got in with the wrong crowd, and had a life filled with drugs, chaos, and misery.

Now Sue and I didn't agree about everything. I'm not just talking about the toilet being seat up or down, or whether the thermostat should be raised or lowered. I'm referring to our taste in music. Sue was always a thinker. She needed to hear music and lyrics that moved her; Bob Dylan, James Taylor, Carol King, Carly Simon, Simon and Garfunkel. These people are poets who happen to sing. Their messages ring loud and clear, painting a beautiful tapestry of melody and words. I still have a doodle that Sue drew while we were talking to each on the phone when we were dating. It was a picture of a cup of steaming hot coffee and some of the vapors condensing into clouds. The clouds spelled out "you're so vain." She was giving me a pictorial representation of the famous Carly Simon hit, "You're So Vain." Sue's concept of what good music had was so contrary to my idea, but we did tolerate each other's style. Give me bubble gum, ala 1910 Fruitgum Company. I could play a medley of their hit, "Simon Says," an infinite number of times. Or The Monkees or Daniel Boone singing "Beautiful Sunday," now that was music to my feeble ears. I didn't need heavy lyrics or stories to be told. I needed what I refer to as "no-brainer" music. I likened myself to the teeny boppers on *American Bandstand* who would give the song they heard a ten because they liked the beat! Pretty shallow, huh? But Sue and I did cross over each other's lines many times to please the other. And the fact of the matter was that we did have lots of music in common. The Beatles, Elton John, and John Denver were just some of the many commonalities that Sue and I shared. These were the artists that would be played on CDs during long car rides, as well as Raffi tunes for the kids, though I actually started to dislike baby belugas after hearing Raffi belt out that song um-teen times.

Actually, the one song that came as close as possible to being our theme song was Elton John's "Crocodile Rock":

I remember when rock was young. Me and Susie had so much fun. We sure did!

Holding hands and skimming stones. Sue lived one block off the Atlantic Ocean in Brighton Beach so skimming stones across the water was easy.

Had an old gold Chevy and a place of my own. Say no more. That was exactly the color and make of a car I had. It was the second car I ever owned, complete with a can opener effect. My front driver's side was ripped open by a garbage truck one morning while I was on my way to work. My parents moved out to Long Island just at the time I got my first teaching job in Brooklyn, so I found a place of my own to be close to my job, as well as close to Sue. I don't think a Suffolk County to Brooklyn romance would have worked out too well.

I never knew me a better time and I guess I never will. You could say that again, Elton!

Oh, lordy momma on Friday nights, Susie wore her dresses tight and Crocodile Rockin' was out of sight. As I mentioned in an earlier chapter, Sue would wear some very snug fitting, great looking outfits, in particular, her orange and blue paisley "extended belt" otherwise known as a skirt! What the heck, she had the body for it, so at times, she showed it off.

I guess I thought of the "Crocodile Rock" not as a dance, but instead representing our lives together, because we really thought the "Crocodile Rock" would last. What was at first a great keepsake song for us became a lasting reminder of what Sue was facing, a life with cancer, and the fear that the "Crocodile Rock" wouldn't last. I used to drive Justin to school, park the car there, then walk home to get a little exercise. I had headphones and my walkman radio to pass the time while strolling. Wouldn't you know it, that every morning I heard that song, and every morning I would break up into tears. To this day, it leaves me with bitter- sweet memories of my time with Sue. We really thought and wanted the "Crocodile Rock" to last forever!

Sounds and Sense Memories

O ne of the great television shows of all time for Sue and me was *M*A*S*H*. It educated you, made you laugh and cry, and brought home some of the tragedies of war. One episode, in particular, dealt with sense memories for Hawkeye. This wounded soldier comes into the 4077 with wet clothing and soaked burlap, which has a particular smell to it because it is soaked in muddy, cloudy water. Hawkeye starts to sneeze uncontrollably after smelling the GI's drenched material. To make a short story long, Dr. Sydney Freeman, camp psychologist, helped Hawkeye to figure out that when he was a kid, his favorite cousin pushed him into a pond and eventually saved him. Hawkeye suppressed this information for years. He had remembered the incident…he fell in on his own and his admired cousin saved the day by rescuing him. And all it took was a smell that triggered these true memories to emerge.

By the way, Sue and I were always in awe as to how Dr. Freeman was able to solve all kinds of psychological problems within thirty minutes. Now that is the type of psychologist I would want, if the need ever arose! Think of all the problems you could have solved and think of all the money you would save—one session and you're cured!

That is the case of smell conjuring up thoughts and memories. There are certain sounds and smells that we become so familiar with in our lives. You know the sound of the flushing water in a toilet, a car screeching to a stop to avoid a major collision, a can opener operating, the booming engines of a jet overhead, the sound and smell of the morning coffee percolating, or the rattling of the trains on the elevated line in Brighton Beach.

Living your life with cancer unfortunately increases the number of familiar sounds and smells that you start to get used to. Since I accompanied Sue to every single test, scan, procedure, and treatment, I learned these sounds and smells as well.

I cannot tell you how many MRIs Sue was subjected to from the time she was diagnosed with cancer, but the one thing that remained constant was the sound of those machines. Primarily, I should explain that these massive scanners work on the principle of magnetic imaging. Sue had to first see if she was able to even be in the room with a machine that could literally rip out from under your skin any magnetic item that might have been implanted in your body. Sue had one such magnet. Before her mastectomy, it was discussed with us by the breast surgeon that while she was out on the operating table, Sue could have a plastic surgeon come in and place a tissue expander in the space vacated by the removed breast. The breast and plastic surgeons assured us that they had done this team work a number of times, and it would make most sense to do it this way. Sue was always afraid of anesthesia and being put out, so this way she could accomplish both procedures while being unconscious only once.

The day arrived and Sue and I went to the hospital along with Sue's dad and my brother. I needed them for moral support while Sue was on the operating table. Sue's dad had already been through this with his wife, Sue's mom, back in 1978. Dad and my brother, Bob, were doing their very best to deflect my thoughts, but as much as they tried, I couldn't stop thinking of Sue and what she was going through. The more I thought, the more I cried. Don't get me wrong; dad and Bob truly served a very valuable purpose that day in the waiting room. I don't think I could have made it through that day without their supportive presence.

An hour or so passed by, and finally, the breast surgeon emerged in her scrubs. I nervously wiped away my tears and asked her how Sue was. She assured me that her part of the job was done. She removed Sue's breast and went to the far margins to be sure that any potential cancerous area was now gone. She put her arm around me and told me that it was a success, and that the plastic surgeon was placing the tissue expander in the cavernous chest area.

An hour passed by and finally the plastic surgeon came

into the room to tell us that everything went great. He explained to me the concept behind a tissue expander, which is basically a balloon with a valve—a *metal* valve that is implanted under the skin. I certainly wasn't thinking at the time of future MRIs to be taken. All I cared about hearing was that Sue was okay and the procedures were successful.

♀♀♀

A further aside about the tissue expander, Sue and I would have to see the plastic surgeon once a month to have saline fluid pumped into the balloon through that metal valve. Apparently, as Sue and I learned, the skin is a very flexible organ of the body. It can expand at intervals. But, like a balloon, put too much air in it and the balloon pops. Same with the skin—too much saline infused in at one time could cause the balloon and the skin to pop. The plastic surgeon was quite funny asking us what type of "look" we wanted Sue to have: Dolly Parton, or Twiggy. Naturally, to emulate the right side breast, we needed the Dolly look and he obliged.

One month later, Sue and I were in the plastic surgeon's office for our routine expansion. He set the machinery up that would pump in the saline. He was always in the room as the procedure was happening. However, about fifteen minutes into it, the doctor was summoned away due to an important call. Sue and I didn't think much of it at the time. Minutes passed, and we both literally see a breast emerging! Apparently, two month's worth of saline poured into the balloon instead of the appropriate single month's supply! Now Sue was very fortunate to be so supple and young, thereby never being in any danger. She was forty years old, and her skin was much more flexible than an older person, so she was able to handle the extra amount of fluid in such a small period of time.

I'll tell you, I have been fortunate to witness three miracles in my life. The first two were the births of Matthew and Justin. The third was the birth of a breast! I marveled at how modern science figured out a way to make a cancer patient feel as "normal" as possible with these implants. It was remarkable! Breast prostheses were still used, but this was as real and part of Sue as possible. We caught many breaks with the balloon as well. We were informed that tissue expanders might last seven to ten years, maximum. Sue's never gave her any problem what so ever, even with the metal valve.

Back to the MRI. The machine looks like a huge "dunkin donut" with a conveyer belt that shifts you into the hole of the donut. If you have claustrophobia, forget it. Your eyes are literally inches from the top of the donut hole. You will never get in one of those things. The worst is when you need an MRI of your brain or head. Sue needed quite a few of those as the cancer spread to her skull. The technicians place your head in a mask and then clamp it down to the conveyer belt so that your head doesn't move at all. You are given music to listen to while the MRI is taking many images of your head.

The music, however, cannot drain out the horrific clanging and rhythmic banging. Each session of pictures could take up to ten minutes, and all you hear is metallic clinging, clanging, and banging. Sounds that I will never forget! They make me remember all of the worry and anxiety of Sue's situation in her life—cancer.

While I was allowed to sit in the room with Sue, all the while I was trying to look into technicians' faces, to figure out what it was that they were seeing on their computer monitors as these images were pumped out. It became a guessing game, and most technicians said the same things when I would ask them how it was going. *Everything is fine, the pictures are clear, and the doctor will be able to read them.* Truly you do want the information given to you by a doctor, not a technician, but the week-long wait for the doctor's report to arrive at our oncologist was sometimes maddening. A little wink from a friendly technician couldn't have hurt. After all, having done their job for years and years, I'm sure that they knew the difference between a good cell and a cancerous one. But be that as it may, most techs played it very cool and didn't let on anything.

Keep in mind that we were not even sure that Sue could step into the MRI room because of her metal tissue expander valve. We were so afraid that the valve was going to become a projectile flying across the room. Thank goodness, for reasons I still don't know to this day, the valve stayed in her chest, never flew out, and never caused any trouble.

Our oncologist's office was separated into examining

rooms and a large chemotherapy room where eight chairs were set up for patients to receive their treatments. In the earlier years, for Sue's first treatments, the chemo was infused by gravity. Years later, when her cancer reemerged, the office used electronic pumps. Those pumps needed to be programmed so that the chemo would enter the patient's system at the correct time interval. Sue and I, being math majors, would check the calibrations on the pump to make sure that the chemo was infused at the appropriate time frame. At the end of the infusion, the pump would beep until a nurse came by to unhook the tubes. That beep, a rather loud sounding "air horn" of a beep, was a consoling factor. It meant that Sue made it through her treatment without a hitch. With each round of chemo came the possibility of negative reactions, which might force a shut down of her treatment. One such reaction happened to Sue when she was on Herceptin. Sue was always pretreated with medicines that would, hopefully, prevent any adverse reactions. She was given Anzemet to prevent nausea, Benadryl to prevent allergic reactions, and saline to flush her system. Sue had had two Herceptin treatments in the previous six weeks with no reaction. The third time, however, was a terrible charm. Sue's windpipe started to swell up causing her to have difficulty breathing. She became cold, clammy, and very uncomfortable. Let me tell you about the wonderful nurses that Sue and I met and really became good friends with. At this time, I got to see them in true "nurse" mode action. The oxygen tank and mask came out, and the oncologist was there in a flash asking Sue questions, observing her, and keeping vigil with her. Sue was given more Benadryl to reduce the swelling in her throat, and after a scary twenty minutes, she was feeling better. We learned a lot that day. First, chemo tends to build up in your system, so just because you have had smooth sailing in previous treatments, it doesn't mean that you can take your next treatment for granted. Secondly, we saw how important it was to have caring professionals who don't panic in crisis situations. They knew what to do, how to do it quickly and efficiently, and never panicked. Knowing that you are in good hands is a comforting factor. After a while, the oncologist gave the nurses the okay to restart the infusion. Sue made it through the rest of that treatment, and when that beep finally sounded, we were quite relieved. That beep was the sound we were waiting to hear!

I always thought about Sue's treatment days as positive days and actually looked forward to them. I would joke with the nurses and say that this was Sue's and my social event for the week. I know that this may sound ridiculous. After all, I wasn't the patient, Sue was, and it was her body being bombarded with deadly chemotherapy. One time, the nurse asked Sue if she was ready for her shot of Procrit (a drug that helps produce red blood cells and thereby helps to keep the red blood cell count at a normal level). I responded by saying, "Yes, we're ready." Sue told the nurse jokingly, "Then give the shot to him!" But I always considered these days as us getting one step closer to normality; one step closer to ridding Sue's body of this insidious cancer. I'm not sure how many of the patients in the chemo room would have agreed with me, but it was what I needed to hang my hat on. If Sue was to be cured, this was the approach we needed to take. Granted, the chemotherapy killed good fast growing cells (like hair cells or the cells lining the throat) as well, but the key was that it was killing the cancerous ones too. And granted, there could have been adverse reactions to the infusion, but the good effects certainly outweighed the bad. Granted that for the next few days after the treatment, Sue would be tired, and she eventually lost all of her hair, but this was okay in my mind. I still had Sue around to talk to, to care for, to do crossword puzzles with, and to share happy moments. It didn't matter what she looked like because I still had my lifetime partner and lover, no matter how she physically appeared.

Later on, as the cancer spread to Sue's skull, a neuro-surgeon decided that radiation to the head could either shrink or eradicate those cancer cells. The cells were located right where the facial nerves enter a microscopic hole in the skull to connect to the brain. It was discussed with our oncologist, and the plan was to have the radiation done for ten consecutive days at a local hospital. Sue, once again, needed to have an MRI done to pinpoint the location on the skull. A three dimensional image was formed of Sue's head, and coordinates were mapped out to the precise place on her skull. This was a true usage of the math that Sue and I taught. Kids would always ask me why they had to learn graphing and coordinates. My answer was always that this was the way you could win at the game Battleship. Now I could say that you need it if you are to become a neurosurgeon!

The radiation room was in the basement of this hospital, and there was only one way to get there—a creaky old elevator which made the same trip over and over again...one flight up then one flight down. That elevator's creak was a unique sound, one of gears meshing together. A little oil would probably have solved the problem, but all I remember is that harsh, ear-bending creak. While Sue was in the radiation room, and I was in the waiting room, I heard that sound seemingly hundreds of times. Yeah, the receptionists had a television blasting in the waiting room to cover the sound of the creak, but it didn't work for me. I wasn't interested in what Regis and Kelly had to say. All I thought of was that each time I heard that sound, it potentially represented another cancer patient. I thought of how sad it was that this problem of cancer is truly an epidemic on Long Island, and that no one was addressing it with the force it truly needed. I thought of how Sue was in that epidemic group and I cried for her.

The sense of smell can also leave one with strong memories as it did for Hawkeye on *M*A*S*H*. As a kid, I remember the smell of hot dogs at the Yankee game, the smell of cotton candy at Coney Island, the smell of popcorn at the movies, and the smell of burning fuel as the massive jets flew over us in Brooklyn. There are certain "cancer-related" smells that conjure up memories as well.

First, and foremost, is the hospital smell. Sue had times when the oncologist wanted her to be admitted to hospitals for various reasons. She needed two blood transfusions because her red count had gone down too low. Sue developed Bell's Palsy, a condition of paralysis to one or both sides of the face. Sue needed Gamma Knife surgery to her head that could only have been performed in the hospital. Yes, Sue frequented hospitals often enough to etch some very strong and lasting sense memories—in particular, odors. Medicinal and antiseptic smells fill the air at a hospital. The floors are mopped with germ-killing ammonia. That smell is intense and knifes through your nostrils.

Now on one hand, you want to smell these smells. It indicates that the staff is trying their best to keep the area bacteria free. On the other hand, it serves as a reminder of where you are and why you need to be there. Sue needed to be there when her oncologist's office couldn't provide the service. They didn't have the capability to give blood transfusions or administer Gamma Knife surgery or radiation. It also meant, at times, that Sue was experiencing a problem that was out of the realm of expertise of our oncologist.

Sue's bout with Bell's Palsy was such an issue. It was very scary the first time that Sue lost facial movement. Naturally, we both thought it was due to the cancer. It happened on a weekend, so we quickly called the emergency number for our oncologist. He suggested that due to Sue's history with cancer, we should get her to the hospital. Bell's Palsy can occur due to many reasons. A virus could latch on to one of the nerves that control muscles and cause it to malfunction, leaving you incapable of closing your eyelid all the way down or unable to smile and move both sides of your mouth symmetrically. It would not be unusual for a cancer patient to experience this viral attack due to the fact that chemotherapy compromises the immune system. As I mentioned earlier, chemo kills both good and bad cells and makes a cancer patient susceptible to air born viruses and bacteria that would not affect non-cancer patients. At the hospital, Sue had an MRI taken of that side of her head and it revealed no tumor. In three months time, Sue regained full use of her muscles, and she was out of the woods—or so we thought. Our oncologist believed that a virus had caused it and it was not cancer related. Unfortunately, it came back a second time. Once again, Sue went to the hospital. At this point, an MRI revealed a tumor near the facial nerve. What initially was confusing the oncologist was now a bit clearer.

You see, Bell's Palsy can also be caused by a tumor pressing on one of those facial nerves that affect muscles. As I mentioned previously, this tumor was located on the skull but pressed up against the facial nerves. It was never determined whether or not it was cancerous, but it didn't matter. It had to be removed, and diminished in size by radiation to that area of Sue's head. Eventually after a longer period of months, the Palsy did subside, and Sue's face was restored to its beauty and natural glory.

The perplexing saga of Sue's Bell's Palsy was that she had it three different times. Part of the problem with rejuvenating facial nerves is that each time a nerve is damaged, it takes a longer recovery time to function again, if it ever does at all. Not to mention that the nerve may come back and branch out in directions other than its original path, thereby leaving the nerve useless and the face in the paralyzed state.

A tumor once again emerged. This third bout left Sue to try a procedure called Gamma Knife surgery. It was done at a hospital on an outpatient basis, where an MRI and three-dimensional mapping of Sue's head was done. After pinpointing the troubled area, Sue was put out so that a "crown" of 210 laser beams could be affixed to her head. It was literally screwed into the skull so that the crown and her head were one. The smell of antiseptic alcohol near the screw incisions was quite evident. It was a pungent odor that filled the room. Once the three-dimensional coordinates of the tumor were established, she was wheeled into the room where the procedure was to be done. The machine looked like an MRI, but without the tremendous noise. As a matter of fact, Sue was asked during her preparation for the laser surgery to bring in her favorite CD. She chose Carly Simon, and while the 210 lasers turned and pivoted into position to blast away at the tumor, Sue was grooving to Carly! Even though the procedure was a success, Sue's paralysis never went away. Future MRIs showed that the tumor was reduced in size, but as we learned ever so painfully, the facial nerve never rejuvenated properly, leaving Sue with a distorted side of her face, and an inability to close her eyelid shut.

I know how Sue felt about how she appeared. She was

embarrassed to have a distorted face—the kind that Picasso would have painted. Going out in public was not high on Sue's priority list. It was also painful for her because her eye could not get the protection it needed. Any wind would dry her eye out, so I purchased all kinds of eye moisteners and drops. Sue used them constantly just to try to keep up with the lack of wetness in the eye. It was just another horror to have to live with, as if cancer wasn't enough.

♋♋♋

Hospitals and their smells will remain in my mind's eye for as long as I live. Hospitals once served as a beautiful reminder of the birth of our two boys. Other than our marriage, those were probably the happiest days of our lives. Now hospitals will always serve as a reminder of the struggles, the pain, the sadness, and the anxiety for Sue living with cancer.

Sue became a living pincushion due to cancer. Before each visit with the oncologist, Sue needed to have a finger stick done. Blood was extracted from the tip of her middle finger, placed in a vile, and then a machine obtained information. The oncologist needed to know Sue's counts of red and white cells and platelets amongst other blood revealing numbers as well. If these numbers were not satisfactory, then a chemo treatment could not be performed. Instead, Sue would get another shot of medicine named Procrit. That was always administered in her upper arm. Its job was to augment the marrow to increase the production of red blood cells so that the following week,

Sue would be able to resume her treatments. All the while, the areas to be punctured were pretreated by the nurses. It was a yellow-orange antiseptic that had an alcoholic smell to it…another odor one doesn't forget.

If these weekly shots weren't enough, Sue had another issue to deal with. It was never established if she was postmenopausal or not. This is important to know because of estrogen. Cancer cells thrive on estrogen. It is produced in many places in a woman's body. The ovaries are the obvious place. Little did we know that it is also manufactured in fat cells. Sue would receive a hormonal shot to the abdomen area named Zoladex. Zoladex interrupts the message from the brain to the ovaries to produce estrogen, thereby shutting down estrogen production. A needle, which appeared to be a foot long, was needed to administer the drug, and Sue never wanted to look at it. She occasionally pumped me for information about the size of the needle, but I never told her. With the area being anesthetized with that odor filled antiseptic and numbing agent, Sue really never felt a thing. This was also due in part to the expertise of our oncology nurses. They knew how to push the needle and the drug in so that Sue would experience little or no pain.

I should mention that along with the good that these drugs do, they could cause some side effects as well. The first time Sue received a shot of Zoladex, we noticed that she experienced joint pain—not severe, but enough for her to need to sit for much of the day. On the third day, Sue's pain was gone. This pattern happened every time she had the shot. So we knew it was coming, expected it, and didn't panic because we knew the routine. Sue was also very tired, some due to the Zoladex, but mainly due to the chemo that she was taking. Again, the good effects well outweighed the bad.

Probably the biggest effect on Sue was the loss of sexual drive. With the estrogen being decreased in her body, she was losing bodily fluids and was as dry as could be. That included tears, saliva, and sweat. Hormonal treatments tend to dehydrate you, making pleasurable things like having sex, very unpleasant. We would read about hundreds of husbands that would abandon their wives because of lack of services due to cancer. And they leave at the time they are needed the most for support, love, and care. This was never a thought in my mind. I can't say it was because of my Christian upbringing because I really wasn't religious. It was in my nature to support and care for my lifelong partner. I'm not looking for accolades here because I was merely doing the right thing. After all, our wedding vows stated "in sickness and in health until death do us part." This was not about my needs. Sue was going through the battle of her life. I just wanted Sue here with me. It didn't matter that she had only one breast, or that she had no hair. All I cared about was that she was here. How dare those other men put their needs ahead of their ailing wives' difficulties. I had and still have to this day no empathy for such men. Talk about sense memories…they leave me with a very bad taste in my mouth!

50 and in the Pink

After ten years of battling this dreaded disease, Sue was to turn fifty years old in July 2002. Even though Sue never said this to me, I think she secretly thought that she would never see the new millennium, let alone the age of fifty. Although Sue was Stage Four at this time, the chemo and hormonal therapy were holding the cancer at bay, and she was feeling well. It was her brainchild to celebrate this momentous occasion in some spectacular fashion. She thought and thought about it and realized the answer was right under her nose.

The color pink is associated with breast cancer. You find it on ribbons, bows, bracelets, pins, and car magnets. I had been wearing a pink breast cancer pin since Sue's initial diagnosis to honor Sue and also to promote awareness of the disease. I cannot tell you how many people commented on the fact that I wore the pin, some asking what it represented and some telling their own story dealing with the disease. Wearing it was really effective to get the message out or to have people's spirits uplifted.

What a great combination…fifty and in the pink! Sue was turning fifty, and she was feeling well so she was "in the pink," health wise. We planned the intricacies of the party: catered food, a huge white tent covering our back yard complete with electric fans attached to the poles holding up the canvas, and Christmas lights adorning all of the trees and shrubs in the yard. I personally blew five circuit breakers overloading the greenery with the lights. But I eventually got it right, and the back yard looked festive. There were eight large round tables covered with pink tablecloths, helium filled balloons—pink of course—floating upward, pink plates and cups, pink plastic dinnerware, pink napkins, pink jugs to hold the soda and pink lemonade, and a huge pink sheet cake.

We invited over one hundred guests, family, and friends. The one slight stipulation for attendance was that every one of the guests must wear something pink…including the guys as well. Some people were quite creative; some dyed their hair pink, some wore pink sashes like a Miss America, and some painted their faces pink. It was great. As for Matthew, Justin, and me, we needed to do something a little different seeing that we were the hosts. We rented pink tuxedos for the evening. Do you know how hard it is to find pink tuxedos… especially in my size? We looked through the Yellow Book for retro tuxedo shops. Remembering back in 1976 when I had no trouble finding a red, white and blue tux, I figured this was going to be easy. Boy, was I wrong! We found only a handful of them on Long Island. We were turned away, and we quickly were losing confidence that we would ever be able to carry out our dream. Finally, we found three such tuxedos at the last store. Matthew and Justin's tuxedos fit just fine. They were skinny enough to fit into a pole if they had to. Mine barely fit around my shoulders and waist, and as for the pants, I couldn't get my leg in both of the pant legs put together. But we were desperate so the kids and I agreed to wear the tux and the pink cummerbund and pink bow tie, but with black pants instead. We changed the laces on our shoes to pink ones, naturally. The three of us made quite an entrance as we followed one another down the back steps of the house. We got a standing ovation for our efforts, as well as a lot of laughs.

As the evening got later, the Christmas lights and the lights in the swimming pool shown brightly, as bright as the smile on Sue's face. Her life with cancer at this time was palatable, and Sue enjoyed being with her family and friends at the party. Included in attendance was Sue's music teacher friend from her days working at the high school, the kid's piano teacher, all three of Sue's sisters, her Dad, friends that she made through her work in the PTA, school colleagues, neighbors that live on our block, and even her oncology nurses.

The last surprise of the evening was just before the birthday cake cutting ceremony. Matthew pulled out a guitar, Justin stood behind a keyboard, and I had a microphone in my hand. The three of us planned to play and sing a little parody of the Beatles song, "She Loves You" to commemorate Sue's fiftieth birthday. The throng accompanied me, Matthew and Justin affirming that Sue was fifty as we all sang in unison proclaiming that benchmark number.

It was truly a memorable party. It was a celebration of life, a celebration of medical miracles, a celebration of the love between Sue and me, and a celebration of the genuine loving care and affection that people had for Sue. Sue, in her own quiet way, was proving that living with cancer was doable. She was living as normal a life as was possible under the circumstances. Sue was, for many, a role model of how to live life to the fullest even though the situation deems it impossible to do so. People were impressed at Sue's positive attitude and overall rosy outlook on life. There is something to be said about having a positive approach and strong mental makeup for battling cancer or any adversity for that matter. Many admired Sue for how she fought the good fight, never complaining, never moaning about her problems. She was always outwardly smiling and enjoying the beauty that life can offer. I too was in awe of how she handled adversity. I often referred to Sue as my hero. Yes, I got to see the other side as well—the inner fears, doubts and tears—but this is where we were good for each other. When one of us needed consoling, the other one was there to help. We understood that we were walking a tightrope with no safety net to catch us if we were to fall, but that was the nature of living with cancer. Sue and I put our faith in our doctors and nurses, the chemotherapy, and the hormonal treatments to keep the inner fears and doubts away.

Fifty and in the pink. Who would have even dared to think of such folly ten years before when Sue was first diagnosed with breast cancer? Sue was demonstrating to us all that cancer was not necessarily a death sentence. At the party, we all raised a glass to toast Sue, wishing her many more "in the pink" parties.

The Port

It was clear by the time Sue's cancer reemerged in her bone marrow that she would have a lifelong need for chemo or hormonal therapy. Unfortunately, Sue was born with very poor veins and arteries. The oncology nurses did their very best to access her circulatory system, but many times, her veins and arteries didn't cooperate. They were very hard to puncture; some were just too small, others too elusive. I guess you could say that the nurses tried in "vein"! The fact was that she could only use her right arm for the injections. Back in 1992, her lymph nodes under her left armpit were removed to see if the cancer had spread. That eliminated any further use of that arm for any medical procedure, including common things like checking blood pressure or drawing blood. Not having a full compliment of lymph nodes could lead to a greater chance of infections, or lymphedema, a swelling of the limb. This made Sue's left arm especially vulnerable if used for any sort of puncturing or pressuring.

Back in 1992 when Sue was first diagnosed, she was on a very aggressive regimen to combat the cancer. She was scheduled for nine months of chemotherapy, the first three months with Adriamycin, the last six with a combination of Methotrexate, Cytoxan, and 5 FU. The Adriamycin was a very powerful chemotherapy medication. It made Sue very tired, and she lost her hair after only a few treatments of it. At one point, her hair could be pulled or combed out leaving tremendous patches of bald spots. She asked me to shave off the rest of it and that struck me hard. It was a terrible image that I will never forget. Clumps of hair, roots and all, just coming off detached from Sue's scalp with no resistance at all. I had seen this once before with our Siberian husky, Shandi. She could be brushed and brushed, and seemingly never stop shedding. Shandi's brush would always have the next round of white and black hair lodged in its bristles after each combing. I was amazed at how the process never ended. Well, the ease at which Sue's hair came off was frightening and never ending as well.

The Adriamycin also caused other damage to Sue. As we knew, chemo killed good cells as well as cancerous ones. After many treatments, month after month of injecting this deadly toxin into her veins, the strength of the drug actually caused her vein to collapse. Sue had a depression on her skin where the vein was originally. You could actually see a ridge in her once rounded forearm due to the collapse. This, along with the fact that she still had many months to go to finish her protocol and that Sue didn't have the greatest set of accessible veins in the world to begin with, caused great concern on the part of the oncologist. Mind you, Sue could only use the right arm because she didn't have a full set of lymph nodes under her left arm. So we were basically stuck (no pun intended!) using whatever good veins were available in the right arm for the infusions.

We somehow made it through the nine months of injections, sometimes struggling to puncture any part of Sue's right side. There were times when the nurses needed to use veins near Sue's knuckles. That is such a tender area of the hand and even though the nurses did their best, it had to have hurt Sue. But it was the only alternative we had.

You can imagine the panic that set in when the cancer reemerged six years later, and Sue needed to receive a new regimen of chemotherapy again. We were not only facing the prospect of the cancer, but also of determining how the chemo was to be administered. We discussed the problem facing us with the oncologist. He suggested surgically placing a mediport under Sue's skin to help in the administration of the chemo.

A mediport, or simply a port, is about the size of a bottle cap for a glass container of soda. It has a membrane that actually seals itself after being punctured with a needle. The other end of it consists of a tube that is implanted into the superior vena cava. The port could be used for multiple purposes, including infusions of chemotherapy and drawing blood. It must be flushed every so often to keep it in proper working order. In Sue's case, that was never an issue because it was used every three weeks for her next round of chemo to be injected. It truly was a lifesaver. We never had to worry about Sue's poor highways of veins and arteries again, we never needed to be concerned about veins collapsing any longer, and we knew that the much needed drugs were entering her system properly through the port.

Sue and I had a meeting with the surgeon who was to perform the implanting of the port. He was a friendly gentleman who convinced us that this was the way for Sue to go. We really didn't need much convincing based on our past experience with infusions in Sue's arm. He showed us a prototypical port. It looked like Tom Thumb's snare drum. It was tiny and the membrane was wrapped tightly around the bottle cap sized plastic ring. To this day, I don't quite understand how the membrane seals itself. Obviously, that was the most critical feature of the port or else blood would flow from the puncture hole as if it were an open wound. The tube coming out from the other side also appeared to be plastic and was small as well. He explained that the plastic tube was fitted into the superior vena cava so the chemo had the best start to its travels throughout the body. The surgeon explained that the procedure to implant the port was done on an outpatient basis, and would result in relatively little discomfort for Sue. Initially, the tube that was placed into Sue's vein was giving her a little pain the first few weeks, but that seemed to go away in time, so the surgeon was true to his words. We were in awe of what science had provided for the cancer patient.

The port ranked high up there in its usefulness.

We used it from that point on and it made a major difference. We became proponents of the port, and we would talk it up to the other cancer patients in the infusion room at the oncologist's office every chance we would get. It was the one of the many inventions that helped Sue to cope in her battle against breast cancer. We also knew that we were lucky that Sue's body was able to handle devices like tissue expanders and ports. Some people were unable to have such procedures performed for various reasons. I think back and wonder how I could be saying that we were lucky. How could anyone who is inflicted with cancer be lucky? Well, we were. We saw other patients in the oncologist's office that were in much worse shape than Sue. Some in motorized wheelchairs because the cancer ate away at their skeletal system so badly that they couldn't stand any longer; some looking so pale and drawn after being ravaged by the ill effects of chemo; and some not being able to raise a limb or keep their heads in an upright position because the cancer and the chemo sapped them of all of their strength and apparent will to fight. Yes, Sue and I saw it all, and we knew that we were lucky. We had good support from our friends and family and another wonderful group of Stage Four cancer survivors that we met on the internet named "the Amazons."

The Amazons

When you think of Amazons, the image that you probably conjure up is a group of savage warriors who would fight to the bitter end to win the battle. What an appropriate name for breast cancer survivors—women who fight every day of their lives to beat this disease, while trying to live as close to normal as possible. Story has it that Amazon women would cut off their breasts before going into battle, partly to demonstrate their toughness and partly so that the breasts wouldn't impede them while waging war.

Sue was always an activist in life. She was involved in the kids' education as a member of the PTA. She was the school's PTA treasurer; a job well suited for a math teacher. Sue was well respected and the community knew the till was in excellent hands—right down to the penny! Sue was also involved in so many other ways in the elementary school. She even worked the soundboard for the school's musicals. When

Matthew belted out "The Sun Will Come Out Tomorrow" in *Annie*, he was heard because of Sue's work at the soundboard. When Justin played the lead part as Charlie Brown in *You're a Good Man, Charlie Brown*, his lines and vocals were heard 'round the world because Sue was of "sound" mind and body at the controls!

♥♥♥

One aside on that play…there was a moment that will be indelibly etched in my mind's eye forever. Justin was auditioning for the Charlie Brown part and was singing just as I happened to enter the auditorium to pick him up. I got there a tad early, so I sat down inconspicuously in a seat halfway back from the stage. Sue and I had just come from taking an MRI because there was a scare that the cancer was acting up and spreading once again. Sue went home after the test because she was exhausted from the mental and emotional strain. There I was sitting in the auditorium seat, with my mind miles away thinking about potential results from the MRI. Justin was aware that his mom had taken a very important test that day, but he wasn't aware that the results took about a week to arrive at the oncologist's office. He spotted me in the sea of seats, and bless him, he tried so hard to continue singing for his beloved role of Charlie, always keeping one eye on the director, but somehow managing to give me a questioned thumbs-up to see if mom was okay. His eyebrows arced upward, his expression very inquisitive and scared as his eyes began to well up. All the while, he attempted to continue singing. You could see how torn up he was inside. Being the good boy he always was at school, he had to continue, but being the caring, sensitive child as well, he needed to know that his mom was okay. I gave him the thumbs-up signal to let him know that everything was all right. That eased his mind and he finished his audition with a flurry. He got the part of Charlie Brown, and the play was a smash hit. It was Justin's facial expression in that moment that I will never forget. His expression showed me how much he loved his mother and how concerned he was for her well-being.

At times, I think back now and wonder if we handled the kids in the best way. Sue and I were always honest with them, but we always tried to put a positive spin on the situation. If they had questions about Sue's status, we would tell them the truth, but would never get into too many details. We didn't want them worrying day after day if Sue was going to die. We wanted the kids to live a normal life being secure that Sue was here for them, and everything was going to be fine. That's the way Sue and I handled Matthew and Justin, probably because that's the way we believed and wanted it to be. We had faith in our doctors and the chemotherapy medicines, and we hoped that things would be fine.

$$\Omega\Omega\Omega$$

Sue was a wiz at the computer. She would get great pleasure in designing playbills for the Cantiques and plays at school, cards and invitations for various parties that we would have, and even in helping me with my grades. She wrote a program that made my life much simpler at marking times. Yes, Sue did it all on the computer, but one of best things that she did, being the activist that she was, was when she sought out support from others in her situation on the computer—other Stage Four breast cancer survivors.

Sue found such a group. These were courageous women whose cancer had spread to other organs of the body just as it had done in Sue. The name of this brave group of women—you guessed it—the Amazons!

Sue actually found these incredible women by chance as she went online to find support groups for Stage Four cancer patients. This particular group has a board where information, questions, and comments were posted daily. It was headed by one of the Stage Four women and she saw to it that the board was run properly and appropriately. The purpose for such a board goes well beyond informational. It is in the true sense of the word a support and comfort zone where Stage Four cancer patients can come to cry, laugh, and lean on one another in good and bad times. For Sue, it was in many cases what the doctor ordered both for her and those that she touched. Sue was always there for the rest of the group members, just as the others were there for Sue. The Amazons would send cyber-chocolate and flowers to those that were feeling down; they would have cyber-pity parties, crying about their lot in life; and they would send cyber-cards of well wishes to those going through particularly bad times. They would share information on which medications or procedures worked and which didn't. Of course, everybody's journey was so different and unique, but it was good to hear from those that had already "been there, done that."

It was through the Amazons that Sue and I learned the "all for one, one for all" attitude from the traits and habits of geese. Geese could be our role models—yes geese. The way of life professed by the Amazons was exactly those rules that were followed in nature by geese:

Fact 1: As each goose flaps its wings, it creates an "uplift" for the birds that follow. By flying in a "V" formation, the whole flock adds 71% greater flying range than if each bird flew alone.

Lesson: People who share a common direction and sense of community can get where they are going quicker and easier because they are traveling on the trust of one another.

Fact 2: When a goose falls out of formation, it suddenly feels the drag and resistance of flying alone. It quickly moves back into formation to take advantage of the lifting power of the bird immediately in front of it.

Lesson: If we have as much sense as a goose, we stay in formation with those headed where we want to go. We are willing to accept their help and give our help to others.

Fact 3: When the lead goose tires, it rotates back into the formation and another goose flies to the point position.

Lesson: It pays to take turns doing the hard tasks and sharing leadership. As with geese, people are interdependent on each other's skills, capabilities, and unique arrangements of gifts, *talents, or resources.*

Fact 4: The geese flying in formation honk to encourage those up front to keep up their speed.

Lesson: We need to make sure our honking is encouraging. In groups where there is encouragement, the production is much greater. The power of encouragement (to stand by one's heart or core values and encourage the heart and core of others) is the quality of honking we seek.

Fact 5: When a goose is sick, wounded, or shot down, two geese drop out of formation and follow it down to help and protect it. They stay with it until it dies or is able to fly again. Then, they launch out with another formation or catch up with the flock.

Lesson: If we have as much sense as geese, we will stand by each other in difficult times as well as when we are strong.

These are qualities to live by, and certainly, they represented the ways of the Amazons.

There were some Amazons that Sue and I got closer to than others; some that became lifelong friends. Due to those close relationships we developed, we all got the brilliant idea to try to meet at some central place—somewhere that we could place the face and body to the words on line. We decided that Penn Station in New York City would be that place. Six Amazons from local areas would all meet at Penn Station.

If you have ever been to Penn Station in New York, you know about the multitude of humanity, the hustle and bustle of everyday life with people racing for trains and its all-around craziness. Sometimes, Penn Station resembles a suddenly-lit room filled with roaches scurrying, trying desperately to find cover and shelter, except the roaches are the commuters doing the same things. How were we ever going to meet up in such chaos and tumult? The six Amazons who agreed to meet there were from different parts of the metropolitan region: one from Westchester, one from Queens, one from Connecticut, one from Manhattan, and two from Long Island (Sue being one of the two). I didn't count even though I was an honorary member and was attending with Sue.

There were no signs, no large pink ribbons, and no fanfare. But somehow, we unbelievably found each other! Normally, in New York City, you just don't go over to a stranger to ask a question for fear of some form of retribution, but there was something about these ladies that made them shine out like beacons—beacons of hope, beacons of care, and beacons of love. We all got into one large circle, hugged, and didn't want to let go. These were our sisters in a battle, in the war against cancer. These were the authors behind the many encouraging words over the Internet. These were the beautiful women who cared for their fellow sisters in times of need and laughed together in times of peace. It was one of the most moving experiences Sue and I ever had. It was meeting people that you felt you knew all your life. These were the true heroes in this world; not the quarterback that can throw a football a million yards or the baseball player that could hit the ball out of the park. No, these were the true heroes that were, for whatever reason, inflicted with cancer and refused to let it beat them. They were the people who carried on as normal a life as possible with their families, keeping that smile on their faces for the rest of the world to see, while taking chemotherapy treatments or facing MRI tests or radiation. That special glow preceded these women. I should have never doubted that we would meet in this sea of humanity called Penn Station.

The six women agreed to go to a corner coffee shop where they could finally talk face to face and become even more acquainted than before. I decided that it would be best if I let them mingle alone (I was the only male there). I left them to talk and I walked around the city streets for a while. During that time, I wanted to show my appreciation for what they had done for Sue in her times of need, so I stopped at a corner flower shop and purchased a pink rose for each of the six women. I got back to the coffee shop where the banter was going on full steam ahead. It was amazing to realize that even though each of the ladies was Stage Four, not a single one traveled similar paths to arrive at that stage. Each woman had an unbelievable story to tell; each one unique in its own way with some being horror stories of misdiagnosis or incorrect treatments. That was the amazing thing—despite the tales of woe—not a single one didn't have a smile on her face, hope in her eyes, and a look of promise for the future. I tell you, these are our heroes! I was in the midst of courageous women, and I was in total awe. I now realized that these flowers weren't only to show my appreciation to each and every one of them, but also to honor their greatness and fortitude.

I handed the roses to each lady, and each one cried and gave me a big hug and thanked me graciously. You see, some of the Amazons didn't have husbands any longer because their men had decided to leave them when they were needed the most during this battle. I think some of them were in awe, and maybe a bit jealous, that Sue had spousal support—thus the tearful reaction. Nevertheless, I was happy and honored to meet these incredible women whom Sue and I were proud to call friends and fellow warriors.

Leaving that day was one of the most difficult things we had to do. We didn't want to say goodbye, we didn't want to leave the clutches of the huge group hug, and we just plain and simple didn't want to leave our friends, comrades, our warriors in battle, our sisters. As each Amazon found her way to the train that would take her back home, tears flowed and voices crumbled. We vowed to make this a semi-annual event, desperately wanting and needing to be next to each other once again soon. The group picture that I took still is in my bookshelf for all to see. That photo demonstrates the different personalities in the group, some more fun loving than others, but all with a common thread, a common bond. It was a beautiful mosaic of Amazons, together at last—as one—strong in unity, all beautiful in their own ways.

I am sure that what went through some of the Amazon's minds was the fact that when you are Stage Four, you don't know how long you can hold out. You don't know if the meds that you're on will be effective for a good long time or if there will be a new drug approved to use when your previous meds begin to fail you. You're not even sure if you will still be alive for the next Amazon get-together. These are the terrible real fears that pervade the thought processes of Stage Four cancer survivors every day. Unfortunately, some of the worst days on the Amazon board were when an announcement had to be written that one of our Amazons was no longer with us. The expression that was used was that she was now "Dancing With The Angels." This is the harsh reality of being connected to beautiful people who are Stage Four...the inevitability of death is great, and it can come quickly or linger on for long periods of time. Just as the path to Stage Four is different, so too is the death process. It was always a sad, depressing day when such an event occurred.

♥♥♥

Sue and I were able to have a second meeting with even more Amazons. This time, we all met at Gilda's Place in Manhattan, an establishment built to honor the life of the comedienne, Gilda Radner of Saturday Night Live fame. She died of ovarian cancer, and while battling the disease, she became an activist, trying to raise funds to build such places to help the women waging the cancer war. The place supplied support groups, a library of valuable books, art classes, and professionals who were there to advise, console, and care for patients.

We all brought food, good stories, and advice for each other. Sue and I met new Amazons this time, as well some of the old friends. It was just like the first meeting with some fresh new faces. It turned out to be a beautiful brunch with all kinds of stories flowing…mainly good stories of hope and encouragement. One of the Amazons that Sue and I had met previously at Penn Station was at Gilda's. She just seemed to be the "life of the party"—the one that people gravitated to. She was bubbly, full of wonderful things to say, and had lots of enthusiasm. Her e-mail name was Lillian Galaxy. I just had to ask why she picked that as her screen name. I knew I was in for an extraordinary response, seeing the type of person she was. She proceeded to lift her shirt up to her bra line exposing her midriff. To my amazement, etched into her skin on her abdomen was a simply gorgeous tattooed galaxy with swirling colors, stars, and planets, all centered on her navel, the sun! It was most remarkable. So ask a silly question, get a wild answer. But because of these Amazon get-togethers, we all got to know each other so very well.

I looked at the faces of the Amazons that day, and it was so good to see these cancer survivors having such a great time with each other. These meetings were good for Sue and for me as well. It allowed us to let our hair down for the afternoon (even though Sue had none at this point in her treatments). It allowed us to see that we were not the only "battlers," but instead, we were one of thousands of Stage Four people doing what we could to live "normally" and that we could enjoy life, even for one brief afternoon. I was so proud to have met all of the sisters, each one an individual in their own right, but each with one common goal—to beat this dreaded disease!

Unfortunately, due to nature of the beast named cancer, little did we know at the time that this was to be the last Amazon meeting for many of the sisters. Word had spread months later via the Amazon board that a number of Amazons were not doing well. Sue and I decided to take a trip to Connecticut where two of the Amazons were failing in health. This would be one of those days that I will never forget. We drove seemingly endless hours to arrive at a hospital where Lillian Galaxy was bedridden. Sue and I had no idea what to expect when we arrived. All I wanted to see was the same vibrant, exuberant, lovely lady that I had met at Penn Station and at Gilda's. We got to the floor that she was on and went into her room when her nurse gave us the okay to do so.

There was Lillian, frail, yellow in color, breathing tubes emanating from her nostrils, an oxygen mask attached to her mouth, and her eyes closed. Sue and I approached her bed where she was lying on her back. We tried to talk to her, but she was on too much morphine. She opened her eyes, but we saw that there was no recognition on her part. I stroked her arm and her forehead to no avail. I was able to literally wrap my thumb and pointer fingers around her wrist nearly twice! That was how much weight she had lost. We spoke to the nurse, and she told us that, at this point in time, her job was merely to keep Lillian comfortable. We kissed her forehead and left.

As Sue and I traveled down in the hospital elevator, we

both broke out in tears, crying for our fellow warrior, Lillian. We got the word on the board a few days later that Lillian was now "Dancing With The Angels." This one visit struck me very hard that day. How could the cancer have moved so quickly to make a once vivacious lady become vegetable-like in a matter of a few weeks? Why did this have to happen to such a wonderful person? What's going to happen to her family? And of course, I thought of Sue. I was scared for her, scared for me, and scared for our children. This one visit hit me squarely between the eyes. Cancer is not a game—it is dead serious. Its unpredictability is terrifying. Lillian did everything her oncologist told her to do, yet she was in such bad shape. I asked myself over and over again: WHY?

Sue and I, still reeling from the visit with Lillian, traveled another seventy miles to see another Amazon who had a recent setback. Her name was Barbara. We arrived at her home to find that she was confined to her bedroom. The family was in the process of installing a motorized chair so that Barbara could get downstairs to join the family at dinner and be with them in rooms other than her bedroom. The cancer had deteriorated her skeletal system so badly that she could no longer stand under her own power. Her cancer had metastasized into her brain as well. She had numerous radiations to the brain to attempt to shrink the tumor and stop the swelling in the brain. She was in much better shape than Lillian that day, and Sue and I had a lovely time chatting with her.

We unfortunately received word that Barbara passed away months later. Barbara's husband wrote a letter to thank us for the visit that day. I'll paraphrase some of it:

> *I'm sorry I didn't get a chance to meet you and Sue face-to-face. We spoke on the phone and e-mailed, and I learned a lot about you both from Barbara. Sue is, indeed, a special person. Her warmth and compassion, and the Amazon network she participated in was amazing.*
>
> *I remember when you and she traveled here to visit Barbara and what that meant to all of us. I wasn't able to be there, but when I got home, Barbara's spirits were better than they'd been in some time. Sue's visit meant so much to her. So did her contact with Barbara by phone and e-mail. It was comforting for her to share feelings and experiences with Sue and the group. It was comforting for my kids and me as well. The Amazons have a special connection, and they take good care of each other.*

Barbara's husband was right on with his description of Sue. She was caring, considerate, and compassionate. I guess you don't go into the field of teaching if you don't have these traits. Sue had all these and more. The one thing that Barbara's husband could not have known however was that both Sue and I got something out of our visits that day. It was therapeutic for us as well to visit our friends and lend a word or two of encouragement. This is the way Sue and I were brought up as kids—help people in need. I have always found that it's easy to be a friend when things are going well, but your true colors as a friend come out when the chips are down and someone needs help desperately. I feel that Sue and I accomplished that by taking the trip to Connecticut that day.

So the Amazon chapter lives on, long after its original members are "Dancing With The Angels". It sometimes takes people a long while to realize that they could stand to use a little help. With the Internet, help is a fingertip away, and the Amazons are living proof. Long live the Amazons, and long live the memory of our fallen sisters!

Idiosyncrasies, OCD, Mystic Powers, and Superstitions

S ue and I always considered ourselves to be logical, concrete, "show it to me and I'll believe it" type of people. After all, we are math people, and math people require solid answers to problems. We don't mind taking differing routes to arrive at the result, but a result is the eventual end to the journey.

Some of that rigidity goes out the window when cancer is involved. As the cancer raged on in Sue's body, our rigidity lessened and lessened. It was amazing to see the amount of flexibility Sue and I were willing to accept to fight cancer. They say that desperate people do desperate things. When you're a Stage Four cancer survivor, you sometimes must resort to desperate things. So we turned to alternative methods as well as chemotherapy and hormonal treatments in the battle against this disease. One such method was Reiki. We had spoken to some of our Amazon friends who used it. They didn't give up on their chemo treatments; instead they supplemented them with Reiki. When we told our oncologist that Sue was going to try Reiki to supplement the chemotherapy, he kind of sloughed it off, saying that it couldn't hurt and if it made her feel better, then do it. So he wasn't against it, but he certainly didn't give it a resounding affirmation. We learned then that each professional puts stock in his or her expertise. The oncologist totally believed in the meds, and that the chemo would help Sue the most. I guess, looking back, to his credit, he had heard of Reiki and he didn't put it down and nix it completely.

Reiki is an eastern approach to calming, settling, and curing areas of your body that have been inflicted with any sort of pain or disease. We were given the name of a wonderful lady who studied Reiki and was totally immersed in its power and abilities to cure. She came to our home, complete with a fold-out table, sheets to place on the table, a pillow, and a CD that had soothing, calming music. She was sincere, caring, and took an interest in Sue's plight almost immediately. We talked about Sue's history of cancer, where it was presently in her body, and which of Sue's organs it was affecting. At this point in time, Sue's cancer had spread to her bones, liver, and bone marrow. The Reiki expert needed to know all about Sue's past and present condition so she could be the most effective while performing her Reiki.

I put on the smooth, soft music very lightly in the background while Sue lay on the table face up. Sue was a little cold, so we placed a blanket over her. I was allowed to sit on the couch that was adjacent to the table. The Reiki expert leaned over Sue's body, never saying a word to either of us. She hovered over Sue and was motioning back and forth over the areas of Sue's body where the cancer had invaded. Back and forth, her hands moving to and fro over Sue's liver, her bones, and her bone marrow. By now, Sue was in such a restful state of mind that she actually fell asleep for a period of time. After about twenty minutes of hovering, the Reiki expert then swept her hands across Sue's entire body, and in a cleaning motion, pushed or brushed away the bad cells. She then cleaned her hands by ringing them out, cleansing them of cancer, and thus cleansing Sue's body as well. She repeated these movements over and over again, then let Sue rest for a while.

Finally Sue awoke, and for whatever reason, she appeared to be at peace and very tranquil. The best way I could describe what I saw was that the Reiki lady served as a lightning rod, attracting all of the good vibes that were in the universe. She then sent those good vibes into Sue's body, attacking the cancerous spots. Then with this cleansing, sweeping motion, she wiped away the cancer from Sue's body. If you were to tell me about this, I would raise my eyebrows, roll my eyes, and I would equate it with voodoo or black magic. But you know what? It really seemed to put Sue at ease. I would never have believed it unless I saw it myself. As I said before, Sue and I are the "show it to me and I'll believe it" kind of people. Well, we saw it, and now we were believers. Hey, I'm well aware it could have been psychosomatic. People that want something to happen kind of make sure that it does happen. I don't know, and frankly, I don't care. All I saw was the result, and both Sue and I were very pleased by it. We continued these sessions, on and off, for a number of years. Each time, the effect was the same—Sue seemed better off having been exposed to Reiki than not. So call it what you want…voodoo, black magic, whatever. It made a believer out of two concrete mathematicians!

♌♌♌

Sue and I had a neighbor who was ultra religious. She was a good friend and every time she would see us taking a walk down the block, she would come out of her home to greet us, say hello, and ask how Sue was doing. One summer, Sue and I didn't see her for weeks and we were naturally very concerned. We found out from other neighbors that she had taken a trip to Israel. Sue and I were relieved to hear that she was okay and had just been vacationing. She eventually came home and knocked on our door. She handed us a teal-colored bottle filled with some liquid. She explained to us that during her trip to the Middle East, she made it a point to go to the river Jordan and fill this bottle with its water. It was supposed to be holy water, and she wanted Sue to have it. She also told us that when times were rough, we were supposed to put some of the water on Sue's body and it will help to cleanse and heal. We did try that a couple of times when results from an MRI were not favorable. We would, once again, try anything because, like chicken soup, it couldn't hurt! Our flexibility to accept non-traditional healing methods was demonstrated once again. I can't say the holy water helped or not, but it made us feel so humble that a "stranger" would do such nice things for us. I still have a quarter of that bottle of water left, and I'll probably use it if the need arises.

❧❧❧

We often hear of stories about positive attitude and acceptance of your situation helping one to live longer. Maybe it has to do with reducing stressors in your life, maybe it's looking for the good in bad situations. I do believe that happier people do live longer. Sue always tried to have that positive, cheerful outlook about her lot in life when in public. I did get to see the other side as well. This was where caregiving really came into play. When Sue was feeling down, I tried my best to talk about the good possibilities, the positive things that we are doing to help us deal with the cancer, whether it was something that the oncologist might have said, or a good result from a test, or just the fact that we were being vigilant when it came to the treatments. It didn't matter. Positivity over negativity was the answer. Some days we were better at accomplishing that than others.

I read somewhere that the author, Norman Cousins, was dying of some disease in his hospital room. His doctors were not holding out much hope for his recovery. As a matter of fact, they thought he had only months to live. Cousin's approach to dealing with this news was to watch and surround himself with a plethora of funny movies and videos. To his doctor's amazement, his positive and cheery attitude kept him alive well beyond the expert's predictions.

People do claim that there is a positive power to humor and hope and creativity, and it directly connects with helping to heal. I too believe it being an eyewitness to Sue. Don't get me wrong—sometimes no matter what you try, the depression and concern is so deep that seemingly nothing will get you out of a funk. I guess the idea is to try to keep those days down to a minimum, if possible!

♌♌♌

One of our best friends had lost her husband to a massive heart attack ten years ago. She told us that she never truly got the chance to say good-bye to him properly. She decided to go to a medium, one who claimed he had the ability to talk to the deceased. She really didn't believe in this kind of thing, just as Sue and I had difficulty believing in Reiki. She happened to be the choreographer for Justin's school play; *You're A Good Man, Charlie Brown*. Now, if you remember from the previous chapter, Justin was the lead in the play, so our friend was working quite closely with Justin everyday. When she knocked on the door of the medium, he answered and opened it. Before she could say a word about anything, the medium turned to her and asked her, "Who is Justin?" This was remarkable in itself because this was not the reason why she was visiting the medium. She explained that she was working closely with him on a school play. The medium claimed that Justin's vibes were very strong. They walked a bit further, and suddenly, he stopped abruptly. He turned to her and asked, "Does Justin's mom have cancer?" Simply unbelievable! She explained Sue's plight to the medium. He then asked her to tell Sue something when she saw her—"Tell her she is going to be okay." This blew Sue and me away. Again, when you are Stage Four, you want to hang your hat on any piece of encouraging news. This was great news. By the way, the medium proceeded to tell her many facts that turned out to be true about her deceased husband. Things like the street where he played ball as a kid or where he worked as a teenager. He also, unfortunately, told her that her cousin, presently afflicted with cancer was not going to make it. True to his word, her cousin did pass away soon after. This guy was something else and right on the money. Don't think for a minute that Sue and I, two people who have trouble accepting this kind of supernatural stuff, grasped onto what he had to say and ran with it. Again, it was a case of it can't hurt us, and instead, it lifted our spirits to know this information. And that it did…for a good long while!

ℒℒℒ

Remember in an earlier chapter I mentioned our trip to California to visit our good friends Lew and Trina? Well, this story takes place the night before Sue was to have her mastectomy. Mind you, we had just been hit between the eyes with this horrible news that Sue had cancer. We couldn't sleep well that night, fidgeting in bed, tossing and turning with anxieties about the next day's operation and our very cloudy future. There was nothing else on our minds other than the impending procedure. Sue and I hadn't heard from Lew or Trina in quite a long while at that point. Well, wouldn't you know it, that night around twelve (nine, California time) the phone rang. I picked it up to hear Trina's voice. She apologized for not telling us sooner, but weeks before, Lew was in a horrific accident. He was driving home from work and a bus slammed into his car, sending him flying out yards away, landing him on the concrete. He was in a coma and the doctors pretty much had given up on any chance of him surviving. Mystically freaky. I then shared my story with her about Sue and her health status. Of all the nights to be telling stories of our respective loved ones being in dire straights, this was not the best evening. On an aside, Lew made it back from his comatose state, miraculously, needing therapy to relearn to eat, walk, talk, use his arms. He alone should be the subject of another book! I wrote earlier that I was fortunate to be a witness to three miracles in my life, the birth of our two kids, and the birth of a breast…throw Lew in there for good measure. And while you're at it, Sue too was a miracle battling all odds to survive and live with cancer.

Everyone loves the fortunes you get after cracking open a Chinese Fortune Cookie. Most of the time they are meaningless proverbs, or general statements that could apply to anybody and everybody. My friend once got one that read, "Disregard your previous fortunes!" Many times I've opened the cookie up to reveal an adage, "Gambling is bad for you" only to read further down the fortune, "Lucky numbers: 4, 7, 9, 15...." But occasionally, just sometimes though, the sayings make you go, "Hmmm...." Almost as if some mystic power directed you to pick that particular cookie and its meaning fits you and your situation to a tee.

When Sue's cancer came back six years later, I wanted to write down our experiences, our emotions, our disappointments, our gut feelings, and our sadness, especially since we had to start all over again battling this dreaded disease. I told Sue that I would write a book one day about the trials and tribulations of a cancer patient and the wide-ranging effects it has on the family and friends of the stricken person. It was a dream at the time that I needed to share with others, a memoir of sorts to commiserate with families in similar situations. Wouldn't you know it, the week of Sue's unfortunate new cancer diagnosis, our family decided to eat Chinese food for supper one evening. With the delivery of food came four fortune cookies. We all picked one. Matthew's and Justin's fortunes were not memorable, but Sue's and mine were significant. Sue's read, "Before you can see the light, you must see the darkness." Wow! *There will be darkness—* obviously the newly found cancer in her bones was as dark as it could get—but more importantly, *there will be light*. Maybe Sue will be cured? Maybe the progression of cancer's march will be held at bay for a good long while? Mine was just as apropos: "You are a lover of words, someday you will write a book." A freaky coincidence or was it fate? Who knows? To this day, I still keep those tiny pieces of paper attached to our refrigerator door.

☙☙☙

Unfortunately, Sue's cancer changed some of things that I would do. These were not life altering changes, just actions that might be attributed to superstition, or OCD (Obsessive Compulsive Disorder). I never went out of my way to accomplish these actions, nor did I hurt anyone doing them. Heck, people never even knew I was doing them as I was doing them. It almost became a fear that if I didn't do these things, Sue would die. Now I know, rationally, that my actions had nothing to do with Sue's well-being, but irrationally, I needed to accomplish them. Some of these actions, I could directly attribute to Sue's cancer. The origin of other actions, I am hard pressed to figure out. I'll share with you the most obvious superstition.

The hospital where Sue was diagnosed having breast cancer back in 1992 was in a little town on the north shore of Long Island. The route we took that morning was to drive on Sunrise Highway to get to the overpass where there is a traffic light leading you onto the Seaford-Oyster Bay Expressway (or

Route 135), where we traveled north to get to the hospital. Now I travel on Sunrise Highway quite often to go east on the island or to visit my mom and dad or my friends. Since that day, September 2, 1992, I vowed to myself that I would never get stopped at a red light at that overpass. I guess, in my irrational mind, I just don't want to be stopped ever again by that route because it stopped Sue's and my life once before. If I see the light is red and am approaching it, I coast until the light turns green, never once putting my foot on the brake. I calculate the distance I need to accomplish this feat without hitting any car in front of me. Irrational? You better believe it; why do I do it then? In my mind, it helped to keep Sue alive, and for us to live and not be stopped in our tracks. Ridiculous, right? Maybe it was my way of controlling an uncontrollable fact that Sue had cancer. Maybe it was my way of saying that we were beaten once before, but we wouldn't be beaten again. I don't know, but I do know that I did it and I will continue to do it. I'm sure that Sigmund Freud would have a ball with me!

I did many other obsessive-compulsive things; some I couldn't explain, others I could. They all started since 1992. All I knew was that doing them harmed no one, and as long as I did them, Sue would be okay. I once asked a doctor about OCD, and he told me that this disorder appeared commonly in high achievers. He claimed that he himself had such actions, and eventually, you kind of outgrow them. I don't know if I'm a high achiever, but I've certainly demonstrated such tendencies.

Sue mentioned to me on certain occasions that she too had some tendencies towards compulsive behavior. She shared with me that on important test days, be it MRI's, cancer blood test marker days (CA 27/29 blood tests), or oncology visit days, she would do certain things to get her through the day. Sue also told me that when she was nervous about a test, she would employ imaging, a technique where you place yourself in a non-threatening situation. She would think of a beach with waves rolling in and out or a sunny day where we'd be walking on the boardwalk or even watching a flight of birds soaring in the sky. This would take her mind off of the test or impending result, a threatening place for her, and put her instead in one of her comfort zones.

Sue was even given a mantra to say by the Reiki lady. Sue would repeat the lines in her mantra to calm herself down and ease her mind. She was also given a prescription for Ativan, a drug that tends to take the edge off and levels off your feelings to help you cope with anxious situations. When we could, Sue and I would take strolls on the boardwalk in Long Beach, appreciating the beautiful scenery, the undulating waves, the clear blue sky, and the brilliance of the sun. Sue, living her early life one block from the Atlantic Ocean at Brighton Beach in Brooklyn, always gravitated to the water. That was definitely her comfort zone, and she and I took full advantage of our proximity to Long Beach's boardwalk as much as we could.

There were many, many ways to help Sue deal with cancer, and she was bright enough and open enough to utilize them when the need arose. The rigid concreteness of two math teachers crumbled under the stress and strain of living with cancer. We learned the hard way that it's okay to ask for and receive help, even if it was out of the ordinary kind of help like Reiki, mediation, imaging, or even compulsive behaviors. We are not super beings that can always handle life's mishaps alone. Aid was there and we used it.

Numerology and Letters

What would a book written by a math teacher be without a chapter on numbers? Unheard of, so here goes. Sue and I always noticed patterns in daily life. For example, did you ever notice how many times you look at a digital clock and see 1:11 or 11:11 as the time? This is not to say that these are the only times that appeared (if that were the case, it would be time to buy a new clock!), but instead, there wasn't a day that went by without us noticing those hours at least once, maybe twice. Or page 111 in a book or flight number 111 or mile marker/exit 111 when you're driving on the road? Now, we are not religious at all, but a friend of mine suggested that this is a biblical notion representing the Holy Trinity (the Father, the Son, and the Holy Ghost). These numbers constantly surrounded us in our lives, not in a good or bad way, just always present. I can't really think of a cancer-related reason why they showed up so often, they just did!

Despite the fact that I taught math, I could never remember important numbers. There are many pneumonic devises used in the teaching of math. (SOH-CAH-TOA representing the sine, cosine and tangent ratios in trigonometry or **PLEASE EXCUSE MY DEAR AUNT SALLY** to represent the order of operations to name a few). Do you recall those? Anyway, telephone numbers, license plate digits and addresses always escaped my memory. So I thought I would apply some of my mathematics teaching techniques to real life! Now that is truly Applied Mathematics!

I know this next statement to be a fact unless someone can disprove me. I believe that Sue and I were the first people to put words to phone numbers. Every huge corporation or business does that nowadays (like 1-800 FLOWERS). When I was dating Sue, I needed some way to remember her very valuable telephone number. When I worked out the lettering behind the digits of her phone, it spelled, "GET GUYS." Not bad for a single, available, ultra attractive girl. We eventually changed all of our friend's numbers into words or some kind of nonsense phrase. After we were married, our home phone number was "MIX TUNA." Try telling a telephone operator back in the early 1970s that your phone number was M-I-X—T-U-N-A. She must have thought that I was *mixed nuts* instead! Mind you, we were doing this in the early 70s, way ahead of our time.

After Sue and I bought our first car as a married couple, our New York license plate began with the letters BCL. We kept that plate as the years went on, and as we purchased new vehicles. After Sue's diagnosis, we noticed an eerie connection to her situation and that those plate letters. BCL stood for something in our eyes—Breast Cancer Lady. Coincidence? The plate always served as a grim reminder of the battle Sue and I faced every day. That license has remained on our car to this day. As I drive around, I notice a lot of New York State license plates beginning with the same three letters and often wonder about the health of the driver.

The number thirteen was a scary number for me. I never watched the "Friday The Thirteenth" movies. I found them to be too bloody and gory. The number didn't hex me, but I guess there is a reason why many hotel chains don't have a thirteenth floor. I always believed that Sue would live a good long normal life span and that we would grow old together, but I always had fears about us reaching the thirteenth year after diagnosis. I never really trusted that year, 2005, and hoped that it would come and go and Sue would be fine. In my irrational fear, I never shared this with her. There was no need to. She was dealing with and beating cancer, and that is all that mattered.

The Five-year Myth

Sue and I truly enjoyed life in the period after the initial nine-month chemotherapy ended. We actually got a little too complacent towards the cancer. Patterns had been set, Sue's hair had reemerged, her subsequent oncology appointments, once every month, were clean and easy. We spent quality time doing things as a family, including trips to amusement parks like Sesame Place and Hershey Park, visiting the Amish country in Pennsylvania, going to movies, and so on. In general, life was good, and Sue and I had passed the dreaded five-year mark since the onset of cancer, so what did we have to worry about?

Just an aside about Sesame Place. We knew that the park was water driven. All the rides had something to do with floating on water, being sent down water flumes, or just cooling yourself off under the water sprinkler or wave pool. Sue and I took precautions to keep our money and valuables dry by placing them in four zip-lock baggies, then holding the plastic containers in my bathing suit pocket. We had a great day with the kids, enjoyed the sun, water, food, the Sesame Street shows down Main Street, and took pictures with all of the characters (my favorite is and always will be Elmo).

Daylight was ebbing so it was time to go home. Our clothes were wet, dampened by the park, but certainly not dampening our spirits. I drove up to the toll booth for the Outerbridge Crossing, a connector between Staten Island and New Jersey. I arrived at the booth, the gate firmly down in its place not allowing any vehicle to pass, and I handed the toll-taker a moist, five-dollar bill. He examined it, then proceeded to close his window. Sue and I thought nothing of it other than he was counting up the appropriate amount of change to hand to me. Two minutes, three minutes elapsed, so I figure something was up. I honked my horn and asked the toll guy to open his window. Mind you, the cars were lining up behind us to get through this toll booth and it was growing in leaps and bounds. He grudgingly opened his window and said to me that since he wasn't quite sure why this money was wet, he would only reimburse me my change after the five-dollar bill dried! Sue and I looked at each other, befuddled, amazed and confused. He didn't believe me that we had just come from a water park. So, he just sat there and waited...and waited. Eventually, when he had had enough "fun" with us, he gave me the change and lifted the gate to let us through. That had to be the most bizarre event that ever happened at a toll booth. This guy obviously took his job a little too seriously!

♌♌♌

The story behind the Stage Four diagnosis was a scary one. Sue, who was always in touch with her body and her feelings, knew that something was amiss after five years of being "cancer-free." She described the sensation as a kind of whooshing in her bones, a feeling she never had experienced before. On the advice of her oncologist, Sue took an x-ray of her skeletal system. The scan results came back with normal results, but Sue knew better. The doctor who read the x-ray suggested that Sue take this one step further seeing that even though it had been five years since cancer cropped up, she was still a Stage One survivor. A bone scan was proper at this time and in order. Sue was going to ask for another test even if this doctor had never suggested any further examination. For the second time in her life, Sue was being proactive about her health. Remember, it was Sue's insistence back in 1992 that she thought she felt something wrong in her breast, despite what the professionals were indicating to her. When it comes down to it, as much as doctors and nurses for the most part care for their patients well-being, it is the patient herself who must go with her feelings, with her gut that may or may not be telling her something.

So, we waited patiently for a phone call so someone

could fill us in on the results. We were partially buoyed by the x-ray findings, but were tentative about the bone scan. I went to work while Sue was home sitting and waiting. As the week moved on, we started to get more and more anxious, thinking that if there was something to be said, someone would have told us by now. During one of my free periods, I called Sue from school. We both agreed that it was time for us to call either the oncologist's office or any other doctor that the report was to be faxed to. First, Sue nervously called our oncologist. The results were in, but he was presently with patients and the front desk secretary said that he would call us back at his first free moment. Here was the mistake that I made that day. I take full blame for it. Sue called me at school on the math department phone. I suggested and pretty much instructed her to call our GP, knowing that she certainly should have a copy of the report as well. So Sue did just that and called the doctor. The doctor put Sue on hold, furthering her heightened state of tenseness. She came back on the phone, and not really thinking to pre-read it, started reading the report verbatim to Sue. I can't imagine the fear that must have been running through Sue at this point. The report indicated that the cancer had spread to six different sites in Sue's bones, at which time she dropped the phone, let out a wailing cry and she shook uncontrollably. The GP tried to settle Sue down, even apologizing to her for being the first to break this horrible news. As it turned out, the doctor misunderstood Sue and thought we had already seen the report.

Sue called me instantly. Unfortunately, the next period

had begun and I was in class. The math department secretary took the phone call and told Sue she would go to retrieve me from class while Sue waited on the other end of the phone. As soon as I saw the secretary at my classroom door, I knew something was up, and I knew it couldn't be good news. I told the kids in the class that I had a family emergency involving my wife, and I needed to leave instantly. As a teacher, you know never to leave a class of students unattended, but I didn't care. They all knew about Sue and her cancer battle from years gone by. Unlike large school districts, news travels quickly in a tiny community and the kids saw my eyes welling up. They knew I had to be with Sue, so they behaved and just simply waited for the bell to ring indicating the end of class. These students were particularly kind, and they knew what to do especially in these circumstances.

I didn't stop back at the office to pick up books, papers, or even my overcoat. I raced out of there to be with Sue, to console her and see us through this. I could barely see the highway due to my tears flowing, impeding my vision. I almost hoped that a State Trooper would catch me speeding and escort me home. All the while, Sue was on our love seat in the living room, rocking to and fro, crying aloud, the uncradled telephone in her lap. I ejected myself from the car once I pulled into the driveway, let myself in, and witnessed a sight I'll never forget for as long as I live. There was Sue, once strong and confident, reduced to rubble, her mind working overtime and she was saying that she was going to die. Six sites of cancer had invaded her bones. What happened to the five-year

171

policy with cancer? After all, the ads and commercials always stated how one was considered cured of the disease if you could make it five years past the initial diagnosis. It sounded like it had spread to all corners of her body, and drowning in cancer, this was it...there was no chance for survival. There could be no more fun times, no more hope for the future. We held each other tightly, not letting go, both of us with stunned empty looks on our faces. Where do we go from here? How do we tell our children? These were the same feelings that Sue and I had encountered back in 1992 when she was first diagnosed...anger, sadness, pity, sorrow, desperation, no way out, gut-wrenching emotions. Someone had just punched us both in the stomach, then proceeded to yank out our insides. Our heads were exploding with negativity. I was so sorry that I wasn't home with Sue to hear the news with her, maybe to soften the blow. I regret that to this day.

We needed to process this new result. Now that Sue was diagnosed as Stage Four, we needed time to get our heads together, to stop reeling from the news and go forward from that point on. Sue's oncologist was so masterful at calming us down and showing us how and where we go from here. We did now what we should have done earlier in the day...let the person who is the expert in the field tell us the news and lead us down a path of hope. Having the GP read the report's findings was overwhelming for her as well. She did not know how bad this diagnosis was or what would be the next steps to take to treat the situation. Sue and I, due to our frustration and impatience, set everyone up for failure—both us and the

GP—by putting a non-expert in an expert's shoes. This is akin to the times Sue and I tried to read the expressions on the faces of the technicians running scans and MRIs. Yes, they had seen it all as well, but it was not their job to interpret the films. Let the people in the expert position do the reading. It took Sue and me a long, long time to get this idea, but we certainly learned our lesson that day.

Our appointment day with the oncologist arrived. Just the fact that the meeting wasn't done immediately should have indicated to us that all was calm; all was and would be under control. We were still visibly shaken by the current situation, but the oncologist laid our fears to rest. This is treatable and winnable. The fact was, though the cancer seemed extensive, it was still only in the bones. He asked us to consider the bones in our bodies as a single organ, and the fact that the cancer was contained only in the bones and not other organs like the liver, or brain, made this only a slight set back. You know, even if he was giving us a song and a dance, it didn't matter. Our doctor was telling us flat out that this could and would be treated and handled. Other than not having cancer in the bones, what better news could we have asked for? He answered every question Sue and I could think of in a calm, quiet demeanor that exuded confidence. After all, he had been there, and done that with many other patients, so this was just "a bump in the road" to him. Despite all good intentions and great care, all you can do is put your faith in the doctors. Definitely ask questions when you are unsure of something, know the names of the drugs you are taking, talk to people in your stage, and by all means, enjoy every single day that you are here if you physically can.

There was no doubt about it, this diagnosis changed Sue's and my life radically. Some form of chemo or hormonal therapy was going to be necessary. Soberly Sue and I had to ready ourselves for this new way of life. We knew the meaning of Stage Four…you stayed on a drug until it eradicated the disease, or more than likely, until it lost its effectiveness, at which point it was on to another medicine. As long as Sue could tolerate the new protocol, we could do this.

Sue used a number of different types of drugs to help her through this next period of time, all the while hoping and praying for eradication, but more so for maintenance, keeping the cancer quiet and dormant. In the future years, the cancer did spread to the liver and the bone marrow, but all the while, the problem was treated with various meds. Cancer, unfortunately, at times is more determined to live than the meds are to kill it. This is why at Stage Four, cancer is treated chronically. When the trouble arises, you take a drug to hold the advance right there. I found a journal that Sue wrote reminding us of the dates of any physical changes, the drugs that were used to combat the problem, and any miscellaneous notes about the protocol:

Breast Cancer History for Susan

September 1992: Diagnosed with *breast cancer*. Had lumpectomy, followed by mastectomy and reconstruction. Four treatments of Adriamycin and eight treatments of CMF. No Evidence of Disease for another five years. Had follow up exams with oncologist.

Fall 1998: Recurrence to _bones_. Tamoxifen failed. Femara, Zoladex, and Aredia administered. Was stable and/or No Evidence of Disease (NED) for two and a half years. Had occasional pain in lower back and down both legs.

May to July 2001: Markers kept rising. Low red blood count (6.0). Had hospital stay and blood transfusion. Two weeks later, bone biopsy at hospital found _bone marrow metastases_.

June 2001: Left jaw went numb. Admitted to Hospital. CT and MRI of head taken. Found _small bone metastasis causing numbness in jaw_. This improved over time.

CT scan was taken to determine protocol. _Liver metastases found_. Spinal tap at hospital. Spinal fluid was clear.

July to September 2001: Herceptin and Taxotere failed. Herceptin and Navelbine failed. Markers up to 351. Had hospital outpatient mini-surgery with port inserted to simplify further chemotherapy infusions.

December 2001: Aromasin, Lupron and Xeloda administered. Side effects of Xeloda included hand/foot syndrome, fatigue, and low platelet counts.

January 2002: Bell's Palsy (facial paralysis) set in. MRI of head taken. Hot spot on skull near dura. Bell's Palsy lasted three weeks.

October 2002: Felt slightly off balance. Brain MRI. No significant change found. Still noted area around dura.

December 2002: Imbalance and slight dizziness unchanged. Ear doctor ordered Electronystagmography

(ENG). Evening of ENG, ear pain followed by Bell's Palsy and very bad dizziness. ENG showed normal results.

January 2003: Another MRI taken in January with no change. The dizziness changed over time. At first, I couldn't walk a straight line or balance myself at all. Within a few weeks I regained my balance (mostly), but was dizzy whenever I turned my head to the right or looked up. This lasted until April, the day of the last Bell's Palsy onset. Bell's Palsy improved very slowly. CA27/29 rose slowly during these months. Because of Bell's improvement and leveling off of tumor maker, we felt that everything was improving.

April 2003: Middle of night. Had bad earache. By 5 a.m. the next morning, Bell's Palsy was back.

May to June 2003: Had brain MRI. Enhancement of cancer in the right auditory canal mildly increased in intensity from Dec 2002 scan. Had consultations with neurologist. Hospital spinal tap was clear.

June to July 2003: Had fourteen brain/skull radiation treatments at hospital. Was under supervision of radiation oncologist.

July 2003: Switched to Doxil. Side effects varied from fatigue, nausea, mouth sores, depression, and anxiety. MRI's were done to determine status of disease. White counts tended to drop and made me more susceptible to infection.

August 2003: Had MRI. Showed that enhancement in the internal auditory canal (IAC) appeared without significant change. Dura-based mets—no change.

October 2003: MRI showed possible slight decrease in

size of one of the dura-based mets. No change in other mets or right IAC.

July 2003 to November 2004: After radiation and over a year of Doxil, hearing in right ear showed improvement, but later had a large drop. Markers dropped from 220 to 72 between July 2003 and August 2004 and then stabilized in the 70s.

August 2004: MRI showed increase in degree of enhancement in right IAC. Could be dural mets or acoustic neuroma.

October 2004: MRI showed a two cm tumor in right auditory canal unchanged since August 2004. Still on Doxil, Aromasin, Lupron, and Aredia.

November 2004: Discussed possibility of Gamma Knife surgery in auditory canal with all doctors. Referred to neurosurgeon. Advised to take a PET scan and wait to decide on surgery. The fear was of further compromising 7th and 8th nerves.

December 2004: Woke up to notice reduced function in the lower right part of the mouth. Unable to say letters clearly, such as "B", "M", and "P." Right eye was excessively dry in recent weeks. I thought it was due to dry weather but now realized that the eye has been drooping a bit more than before and unable to wink right eye at all. Additionally, the left side of the chin and lower lip was a bit tingly and numb as well as the left side of the tongue. Admitted to ER at hospital. Saw oncologist and neurologist. Was put on Decadron, 4 mg every 4 hours with saline flush to prevent urinary tract infection

(UTI). Took MRI of brain and results showed no change from the previous MRI. Released on Dec 9th with appointment made to see neurologist. Decadron continued at home by pill (4 mg twice a day). Other symptoms included sinus-like puffiness. Took Sudafed as needed as well as Ativan.

December 2004: Met with neurologist. He suggested no spinal tap based on the facts that palsy had responded in time. No change on MRI. Tumor markers remained stable. Maybe prone to Palsy at this time of year. Take follow up MRI in two months. Met with neurosurgeon. Suggested that we wait and see. No Gamma Knife surgery, rather small directed dosages of radiation at later time. He was concerned about the proximity of the tumor to the nearby nerves and the brain stem.

December 2004: Slightly increased sensation of tingle on left side (other side) of face.

December 2004: Spinal Tap done by neurologist. Results showed no cancer activity in the spinal fluid. We have full reports. Tumor markers rose to 95 from 73. Will repeat in a month. Tingling came and went on the left side. Still some numbness on the left side of the chin. Increased discomfort in the right eye.

January 2005: Oncologist suggested seeing neurologist for a consultation as to further treatment. He felt spot radiation or Gamma Knife would not do any further damage to the nerves that are already damaged, but he deferred to the judgment of the neurologists. Neurosurgeon's concerns should be noted, however.

January 2005: Had eye exam. Concern was excessive dry eye due to Bell's Palsy and chronic dry eye possibly from the medications. Suggested cosmetic surgery to partially close the lids at the outer corner of the right eye. Pictures indicated a small area in the blood vessel causing blurriness to the right eye. Did not appear to be related to cancer. More likely due to low platelets. I will consult with their retina specialist and optical cosmetic surgeon within a few weeks.

Visited with GP. Everything normal except for slightly high cholesterol. Began to feel a little flutter. Mentioned to oncologist and he suggested a halter monitor. Also, red spot on my chest, supposedly from Doxil, has gotten worse. Oncologist recommended seeing a dermatologist.

January 2005: Visited with dermatologist and did biopsy of the chest spot. Several days later, report showed it was a squamous cell carcinoma. He took a biopsy of a nearby spot that showed to be clear.

January 2005: Bone scan. Radiologist read it instantly and said there was tremendous improvement from 2001. He then took a closer scan and an x-ray. He did not find any jaw metastases.

February 2005: Went to oncologist. Decision was to stop Doxil, Lupron, and Aromasin due to increase in tumor markers 20 points to 92 and continued symptoms. Took first treatment of Faslodex. Gemzar to follow after Gamma Knife procedure.

February 2005: Gamma Knife performed at hospital by neurosurgeons. MRI prior to procedure showed a "floating" tumor in the sinus cavity, possibly explaining left jaw numbness. Tumor in right IAC and left sinus cavity treated with Gamma.

The log continued on and on, but I think you can see the frequency of visits increased, the roller coaster ride continued from good news, bad news, and visa versa, and more importantly, the stakes got higher. The change from Stage One to Four is monumental. Life became apprehensive visits to the many specialists, week after week, month after month, yet we did live a "normal" life. I know that sounds hard to believe, but Sue and I went out for dinners and movies when her health allowed it, and we definitely enjoyed holiday seasons with the family. Granted, we used our house as our sanctuary and needed to stay within its confines much of the time due to Sue's dry eyes and Bell's Palsy problem. This actually gave us the quality time you hear about. We did crossword puzzles and jumbles (let me clarify that, Sue did crossword puzzles and jumbles while I lagged way behind), we sat together and talked many times about her fears, we laughed and cried together, or we just simply watched television, hand in hand propped up in bed. This was our normality, and we really needed each other and enjoyed each other's company.

I do remember on many occasions Sue telling me to go out and do things with my friends. She referred to them as "play dates," but I couldn't leave her. Inwardly, I didn't know how much time she had left (even though, not one doctor ever said anything like that to me!). In retrospect, I see now Sue's wisdom shining through. It was not good for me to become so one-tracked, so single-minded because even though it was never discussed, there would come a time when she was no longer here. Then what? My identity as caregiver would be shattered and I would then have no identity. I'd be lost in a world without my only reason to live. I never did a good job at resolving that issue, but I did what I thought I needed to do, and most importantly, what was the Christian thing to do. Maybe hidden in me was some religiousness!

The number of drugs Sue used was immense, and one of the fears you have at Stage Four is that eventually, you will run out of them. The scientists couldn't produce them fast enough to suit us. With all this, you must be thinking how could any person have the strength to face each day. Well, Sue did. Not only did she face it, but she took it on head long, with a smile, with dignity, and with the class I knew she had…traits that endeared her to me when we first met. I fell in love with her then, and I was even more in love with her and in awe of her now.

After the cancer found its way to Sue's skull region, the situation became more serious. Earlier, there were bone metastases discovered in the jaw. We were now nearer the brain even though the situation was still considered as bone metastases. Then liver metastases. Everything was exploding in our faces. I couldn't do it any more, be teacher and caregiver. It was at that point that I needed to make a very important, yet "no-brainer", decision and it explains why I was able to spend time with Sue.

I told my school district that I could no longer work

because I needed to be with Sue. I did not want to cheat the students. My concentration on their well-being would have been greatly compromised because all I'd be thinking about was Sue and her condition. So I left the school district where I was employed for twenty-five years. I was not at retirement age but that didn't matter. I knew what I needed to do. The district ended up working with me, helping Sue and me in any way it could. My colleagues told me to consider the aid payback for all of the great years and fine dedication I showed to the district. I guess I was able to accept help if I thought of it in those terms. A year later, my school district honored me at a Board Meeting by retiring me. I couldn't attend because of Sue's health, but I did send a letter to be read in lieu of my appearance:

Dear Parkland Administration, Board Members, Colleagues and Friends,

I want to thank the District for honoring me tonight. Unfortunately, due to health issues, I am unable to attend. I did, however, want to thank the school district for twenty-five wonderful years. I will never forget the opportunity the district gave me back in 1977. I was just starting to develop my skills as a teacher, and with the help of many people, I grew into a professional. I did my best every day to influence young minds, teach them to think critically, and hopefully, to have fun learning.

It truly has been my pleasure to be associated with the district. The wonderful people in central administration, the members of the school board, parents, principals, assistant principals, the many students that I had the joy of teaching, and my great colleagues…I have always considered you all as my family. It has been my privilege to know you.

I will never forget how the district has treated my wife and me in our moments of need. The support, the comforting words, and the prayers have helped us to cope during these past ten years. The time that the district has afforded me to be at my wife's side was, and is, greatly appreciated. This is truly a district that cares for its members, from the superintendent on down. I will never be able to express in words the full extent of my gratitude for what my compassionate school district family has done for us.

It is unfortunate that health issues involving my wife and me have forced me to prematurely leave the profession and district I love so much. I still have that childlike enthusiasm for teaching that I had twenty-five years ago, but at this point in time, I have a new calling in life—being there for Susan, which I also approach with hope and enthusiasm for the future.

I have lived a charmed life and I consider myself blessed to have all of you part of it. Thank you very much. Sincerely,
Joe Russo

It was at this time that I sought professional help to cope with this ever-growing, all-encompassing issue. I was breaking down mentally and physically. It was too much to handle by myself anymore. Sue was much stronger than I was. To this day, I don't know how she managed each day to move forward seeing what she faced. Was it her acceptance of her situation that I couldn't bring myself to face? Was it her ability to realize eventualities that I couldn't and wouldn't admit to? Maybe Sue's contact with the Amazons was enough to bolster her everyday? I don't know, but I saw first-hand what Sue's cancer was doing to me. I also vowed to myself and to her, from day one of her diagnosis back in 1992, that I would remain strong for her. A weakened Joe was no good to Sue, and I didn't want to turn this into the "Joe Show." This was all about Sue and her healing. So after nine years of "macho" self-dealing, I reluctantly gave in to see a social worker/ counselor. Coming from my prudish, sheltered up-bringing, this could only mean one thing…I was going crazy because only the infirmed needed counseling. This was a hard concept for me to overcome, but I was at my wits end. I desperately needed aid to cope, to stop the crumbling, emptiness I felt inside everyday, to halt the spread of dread. Some very hard hitting, gut-wrenching sessions left me at times in worse shape than before going in. The therapist never needed to look at his clock on the wall behind me in the room. He knew the hour session was up just about the time I wiped him out of his entire tissue box of Kleenex every week! Even though very painful at times, these appointments did help me to face the present situation so I could help Sue in the future. I regretted that I didn't do this sooner. I'm so glad for myself and mainly for Sue that I saw the light.

So what did we get out of this five-year myth thing? Stay vigilant and never get complacent when it comes to cancer. This five-year cancer-free marker may work for the majority of people, but it was certainly not 100% correct for all. Being aware and taking precautions, unfortunately, may not be enough to stop the insidious march of cancer, but it's the only control that you do have in an otherwise uncontrollable situation. It empowers you, you are not just sitting, idly watching the devastation that cancer performs on the cells of a body. Sue could have thrown her hands straight up to the sky and said, "I give up!" Instead she said, "Never give up, never surrender!" If you notice on some of the journal entries, Sue wrote that she took Ativan. This little pill helped her to get instant relief from fear, terror, or impending doom. When she felt down and anxious, she took it and Ativan made quite a difference.

My purpose here is not to scare people but merely to relate what happened to Sue and me. The thing I've noted from talking to the Amazons, other patients in the oncology office, and reading articles about cancer is that everyone's cancer path is different. Sue's was unique in the sense that the cancer took hold near the jaw and ear thus causing Bell's Palsy, dizziness, and impaired hearing. It also forced us to have to go see so many wonderful, caring specialists from all different fields. Sue's case was an enigma, but through it all she championed her cause of awareness and encouraged those afflicted with cancer to keep their eyes and ears open. She advised them to get in touch with their feelings and their own body because they ultimately would be the best judge. Remember, that back in 1992, it was her persistence that prompted doctors to perform a needle biopsy despite the non-findings of a mammogram. Sue knew first hand the importance of being proactive instead of reactive and she beaconed that message every chance she had.

9-11 Morning

I t was one week into my premature retirement. I had called my school district earlier in July, informing them that I could no longer perform my duties as a teacher to the standards I had set for myself. I could no longer "fool" my students and colleagues into thinking that my thoughts were 100% with them every day. I didn't want to compromise the school, and I certainly didn't want to compromise my time with Sue.

Being at home with Sue, 24/7, was a brand new experience. Matthew was at college, beginning his freshman year at Princeton, and Justin was in his "senior" year at the middle school. Sue and I basically had an "empty nest." But there was one unwanted visitor in our lives, filling the void, not wanting to leave our premises, usurping most, if not all, of our time and concern—cancer. Part of the reason why I needed to be here with Sue was because of days like this particular one. Days like this were occurring more and more frequently, and I needed to support Sue and Sue needed to support me.

Sue and I were propped up in our bed staring into space, silence engulfing the room. In the preceding days, Sue had taken a CA 27/29 cancer blood test marker exam. From the previous test, the trend was that the numbers were climbing which indicated that once again the cancer was on the move. She had just been placed on a new regimen of drugs three months ago, and this was to be the first sign post for everyone involved, i.e. were the new chemos working? Did they stop the steep slope of ineffectiveness of the former drugs? If they didn't achieve their goal, what was next? How many more protocols were left to try? We were so nervous about our visit to the oncology office that day because of all these unanswered questions floating around in our heads. So, there we were, sitting up, blankly looking forward at the bedroom wall opposite us and thinking and waiting and thinking some more.

It had been too long since we could take a proverbial deep breath and once again feel good about life. We knew the importance and severity of each test result at this stage in the game; we knew where we stood, it's just neither Sue nor I wanted to say anything. That empty pit feeling hit us right in the stomach as we started thinking about the worst case scenarios that morning. Our future was once again cloudy, unsure, and ominous; we desperately needed a good result.

The phone rang at about 8:50 a.m. Who could that be?

Was it the oncologist's office prepping us for bad news? Was it some solicitor asking us to donate money for the umpteenth time to his organization? Sue was frozen in her position, so it was my job to answer the phone. It was Sue's little sister calling us from Florida.

"Do you believe what's going on?" she exclaimed.

I respond, "What are you talking about? Sue and I are in our own little world worrying about today's blood test results".

"You've got to put on your television…you are not going to believe what's on!"

We put on any channel quickly to witness one of the Twin Towers burning at what appeared to be two-thirds up its massive structure. Terri and I speculated as to the cause of this tragedy for some time on the phone, then suddenly, to our further disbelief, the next Tower was ablaze as well a little after 9 a.m. I thanked Terri for informing us and I hung up the phone. We were fixed, glued to the television screen watching in amazement. It was as if we were witnessing a video game being virtually played out on the screen; it was utterly indescribable to see the damage, the confusion, the chaos, the tragedy unfolding before our eyes. We tried to make some sense of it. Sue and I thought instantly of Matthew, alone at Princeton University. Just two days prior to this, Sue and I had delivered Matthew there and set him up in his dorm room. That day, Sue was not feeling well at all, and even though she wanted to accompany us to his initial day of school, she was listless and tired. The recent chemo treatment had taken its toll on her, but like the trouper she was, she stood in registration lines, picked up keys to Matthew's room, and even took a few items out of the van and lugged them into his room.

We called Matthew at his dorm. We needed to make sure that he was safe and sound. It was comforting, in the midst of panic in the streets of New York, to hear Matthew's voice. Justin was at the middle school. We called there to make sure that the school was secure. The administration assured us that the student body and staff were protected, and Justin would be fine. Next, we started to think of other members of the family that might be in the area of the once majestic Twin Towers. Sue's cousin worked in the World Trade Center building one day each week, and we hoped and prayed it wasn't Tuesday. We did some calling around to find out that she was not in the Twin Towers that day. It seemed as if our immediate family was safe, but then reality set in. Today we had a potentially course-changing medical result staring us in the face in a few hours at the oncologist's office. It was almost too much to bear…the future of America and our future as well. It was all crashing down on us as we watched and thought; the crumbling of our world on so many different levels as Sue and I knew it.

Reporters scrambled to get eye-witness accounts of the events. I remember one such person stating that, "Everything reminded me of a huge funeral, people crying, sad. It gave me a cold feeling." I couldn't help thinking that these thoughts pervaded my mind as well, but for different reasons.

We had to leave the television reports behind and travel

to the doctor's office. All the way there, we were wondering what to expect when we arrived. The waiting room was abuzz with the news of the day, patients bewildered and perplexed more over the tragedy than their own reason for their visit to the oncologist. Sue and I were doubly troubled, thinking about the appointment and its findings as well as the world's happenings.

It was time. We were called into one of the three examination rooms, and as per usual, Sue was asked to put a gown on so that the doctor could see her. Time ticked away, anxiety festered, and then we heard three gentle raps on the door. That was the routine for all of our visits throughout the years. The doctor came in, and we could read his face instantly. Sue let out an "Oh no" as he proceeded to tell us what we didn't want to hear—that the cancer markers had continued to climb, so the present protocol needed to be scrapped. He always came in with a new plan, however, because we still had untried drugs to use. We were disappointed because we just lost the use of Herceptin and Taxotere as viable choices, but since previous studies showed that Herceptin when used in conjunction with Navelbine had good success rates, the oncologist suggested that approach. Each disappointment got Sue and me one step closer to having no choices left which would spell disaster for us.

The rest of Sue's physical went well, so it was off to the treatment room to start the new concoction. With new drugs come potentially new problems. The oncologist, Sue, and I didn't know how her body would react to the new approach, so once again uncertainty set in. A television was set up in the treatment room so everyone could keep tabs on the world's situation. By this time, the Towers had collapsed, the Pentagon had been struck, and stories were beginning to emerge about the bravery of the passengers on the fourth flight that crashed in the fields of Pennsylvania. The confusion and the speculations about the events of the day paralleled the confusion and speculations that Sue and I had about the new drugs and our health future. The treatment had no immediate side effects, but in the next few days, it did wipe Sue out, sapping her of her strength and all she wanted to do was put her head down and rest.

Questions remained: Would this combination of medications slow down the progression of cancer? Would it lead to other side effects in future weeks after the buildup of many weeks of treatment? Could Sue get a good long run of months with these new drugs, or dare I be greedy and ask for years? If these didn't work for whatever reason, what would be next? How many medications and combinations were left to try? Were there new, untested chemotherapies on the horizon almost ready for U.S. government approval? This feeling of more questions than answers mimicked the citizens of our country and the world with the 9-11 catastrophes.

This day became a turning point for America in how it deals with terrorism. 9-11 was also a turning point, albeit a negative one, for us and our struggles against cancer. America's freedom was being tested and pushed to great limits as was Sue's and my freedom from cancer. You couldn't help thinking that day that terrorism was winning the war, and we couldn't help but think that cancer was winning the war in Sue as well. It was a lost day for EVERYBODY!

One aside, September 11th is the 254th day of the year leaving 111 days in the year. There it is again…111.

The Oprah Letter

S ue had had enough after a while. She saw all the ads on television and heard it all on the radio about Stage One cancer survivors. Yes, she had empathy with their plights, but the truth of the matter is that there are more Stage Four survivors now because of the brand new drugs being used. Stage Four was no longer a death sentence. Instead, cancer at that level was treated as a chronic disease; you use the chemo and hormonal therapies that are at your disposal, and when and if it loses its effectiveness, you go on to the next drug, picking the one so that it will kill cancer cells from a different approach from the last protocol. The key is to keep producing more and more drugs because if you run out of them, you can't go back to previously tried ones. The cancer will have mutated too much and will have actually learned to survive with the chemo that once annihilated it.

So Sue, being a fighter and a leader in causes, took it upon herself to speak on behalf of the thousands and thousands of women who were truly the Stage Four silent majority. She composed this letter and sent it off to Oprah Winfrey's staff, not looking for the limelight herself, but instead looking to be heard. Unfortunately, we never received a response back from the show, but that didn't deter Sue. If anything, that made her resolve stronger. Be prepared with a bunch of boxes of Kleenex. This was a moving and powerful plea to be heard!

Stage Four Breast Cancer:
A New Generation of Cancer Survivors

Dear Doctors and Drug Companies,

We've all heard many stories about the brave women who have faced and beaten breast cancer with the help of early detection and modern treatments. I applaud each and every one of these women for her courageous fight in confronting her disease and taking all appropriate action to get well again.

For many women, however, cancer returns, even if it was treated early. For some it happens very quickly, and for others it can happen well past the desired five-year mark, which defines them as "survivors" who have beaten cancer. For me, it was after six cancer-free years that I was forced to resume my battle. There are thousands of us, and some of us have been lucky to find each other through support groups. I have become a member of the family of hundreds of women living with recurrent, metastatic breast cancer on an online bulletin board. My objective in writing this article is to bring

about "Advanced Cancer Awareness." I would like the public
to be aware of the issues facing the many people who are living
every day with cancer.

Breast cancer can recur to the same or other breast or
anywhere in the body, but most often it recurs to the bones,
liver, lungs, or brain. There are a large number of treatments
available today that were unheard of years ago. Some attack the
cancer hormonally; some target specific substances in certain
cancer cells. Radiation and chemotherapy are still most widely
used. There are many new types of chemotherapy available
today, and thankfully, new medicines that help us to deal with
the adverse effects of chemotherapy. When breast cancer recurs
to a distant site (metastasis), most likely the patient will be
on one treatment or another for the rest of her life. Because
of these terrific new advancements in the treatment of breast
cancer, there is now a huge population of cancer survivors—
people living with and battling breast cancer for many years.
It is difficult to think of ourselves as "survivors" since we
have not beaten the disease. We are undergoing continuous
treatment while raising families, working, and struggling to
live as normally as possible.

Some of the women I hear from online are as young as
thirty-two; others much older. Many have young children to
take care of; some are divorced or unable to work; each of us is
battling cancer while trying to have a normal life with family,
friends, work, and recreation. We have our good days and our
bad ones. There can be months when we are able to enjoy life
and not think about cancer every day and then many months

when cancer pervades our every thought. How long will this treatment work? What medications will I be taking next? Will I have difficult side effects? How are my husband and children affected by my illness? What if I die? This disease taints every aspect of our lives. Our schedules are centered around doctor visits, scans, and treatments. We are always tired or feeling some kind of side effect. We are very lonely because although our friends and family love us very much, they often don't know what they can do to help.

The media has publicized two groups of cancer patients: those who have beaten the disease and those who have lost their battle. We never hear about the hundreds of thousands of people who are living with cancer every day. I encourage celebrities and well-known people who are living with metastatic cancer to come out and talk about their battles. We know there is no cure for cancer. We know that eventually, every cancer treatment stops working because the quickly dividing cancer cells mutate and learn to beat the treatment. We live each day hanging on to the hope that one more new treatment will come along soon, or that one day there will be a real cure. Our parents' generation lived very short lives after a cancer diagnosis. Hopefully our children's generation will be cured shortly after a diagnosis, but our generation is living with the disease and learning to keep it at bay while discovering more and more treatments, but we are also guinea pigs in the learning process.

Most people think of survivors as those who have been through a traumatic experience and come through the other

side as victors. We are all survivors. We have not given up by crawling under the covers and letting our cancer beat us. We are fighting every day to survive by continuing treatment despite the side effects and by entering clinical trials to help develop even better medications for our future sisters. We continue our fight, take care of our families, and try to put on a happy face for all those around us.
Not To Be Forgotten Stage Four Survivor,
Susan

All I can say is this was an amazing, gut-wrenching letter from an incredibly beautiful, courageous woman, my wife, Susan. Good for you, Sue, you presented your cause well. We all heard you loud and perfectly clear!

Our Healing Movies

Sue and I used movies as an escape from the realities of cancer. We loved to laugh, and naturally got attracted to funny flicks. They say that laughter is a great cure. It leads to positive feelings, and we believed it helped in the healing process. If you come to our house, you'll encounter a collection of hilarious and feel-good movies. From Peter Sellers' *Pink Panther* compilation to Marx Brothers classics, we amassed them all.

In a medley of fantastic films a few truly stood out as our all time favorites. *Galaxy Quest* was one of them. The concept of a far-reaching civilization patterning their every move and breath on a *Star Trek* type program on Earth was genius. The television show, *Galaxy Quest,* had been in reruns for years, and the actors were now subjected to appearances at sci-fi conventions. They grudgingly shook hands and gave autographs. A civilization consisting of alien rebels pick up the broadcasts of *Galaxy Quest* reruns and aren't aware that it's just fiction. They travel to Earth to get help from the *Galaxy Quest* crew. They meet the cast of *Galaxy Quest* who think the aliens are just other weird dressing convention goers. However, the cast soon realizes that they are not being hired for another autograph-signing session, but instead to help the aliens in a real outer space life or death rescue mission. The byplay between the actors (Tim Allen and Alan Rickman in particular) had Sue and me in stitches.

Sue had a signature line when she ended her e-mails, and it came from *Galaxy Quest*. The crew, when in trouble and in need of a rallying cry would shout out, "Never give up, never surrender." Boy, this couldn't be any closer to Sue's attitude about her bout with cancer. She would get great feedback from those who would read her signature line. This was truly the way to approach the disease—never give up, never surrender!

Probably, the most poignant movie we loved was *Mr. Holland's Opus*. It had many levels of connections for us. On the surface level, it was about a teacher who played the piano. As you are aware by now, both Sue and I taught, and both Sue and the boys played classical piano.

But there was so much more that we related to in the movie. It is a story about a musician whose ultimate goal in life is to produce an opus that would make him a household name. Unfortunately, it was taking him a very long time to produce this epic musical score, and the everyday bills kept piling up. He accepts a job as a music teacher in a local high school just to earn a much needed salary. What happens after that is amazing. Mr. Holland evolves into a teacher who, through his music classes, makes profound differences in students' lives by showing care, love, and concern. Every year, his music department's program is threatened by school budget cuts. Mr. Holland has to fight long and hard to maintain his music department knowing the positive impact it has made on his students.

An interesting secondary theme emerges when he and his wife give birth to a deaf child. Mr. Holland is greatly troubled by this because he feels that he can't share the very essence of his being with his "impaired" son. He becomes distant and angry with his son, often times not even acknowledging his presence. Oddly, the death of John Lennon miraculously changes their relationship for the better. That one event helps Mr. Holland realize how short life is and how truly important his family is to him. He finds ways to communicate not only through music, but through the use of sign language and visual aids. This breakthrough not only allows him to communicate with his son, but many deaf students he would have never reached.

His love for teaching and adjustments he needed to make to relate to his having a deaf son, paralleled our lives. We had no idea that cancer was in our future, just as Mr. Holland didn't know that his son was going to be born deaf. Yet adjustments, changes in the game plan were necessary, and both parties did what was needed to make a bad situation better. Sue also was a teacher that made a difference in kids' lives. She, a Mrs.

Holland type, was revered and respected by her students and loved by her colleagues.

The last movie I'll mention is a family favorite. It has become the movie we all sit down and watch at Christmas time. *It's a Wonderful Life* with Jimmy Stewart and Donna Reed is a timeless classic, similar in many ways to *Mr. Holland's Opus*, it demonstrates how much of a difference a person makes in the world.

The movie illustrates in a sad, poignant, yet comedic way what life would be like if one had never been born. It shows how many people we all touch in our lives and how we all positively affect others. George Bailey learns that lesson the hard way. His guardian angel, Clarence, gives George the chance to see how different life would be if he were never born.

The little quaint town of Bedford Falls would become a haven for crooks, strip joints, and gambling houses because it would be overrun by the "dirty" money of the town's mean old miser, Mr. Potter. George always fought Mr. Potter's wishes to take over the town by keeping his tiny Building and Loan Company afloat. But without George and his concern for others, the town would fall like a house of cards. George's friends would become destitute without him, some would have to live on the street and others would be shunned by ruthless unsavory town members. They needed George's trust and concern to advance them desperately needed money to survive. Even George's wife Mary would never marry, but instead become an old maid, George's brother would die in the frozen pond as a kid because George would not be there to save him. You get the idea.

We all have an affect on other people just by our mere presence; some of us even effect a more profound change in others. Nevertheless, the world without us would create a major void with consequences we could not comprehend during our lifetimes. George was lucky. He got the opportunity to see those consequences. Once he realized the positive domino effect his life had on others, he viewed life's problems differently. George's failing Business and Loan Company, his possible jail sentence, even his drafty, cold, old home with its loose stair spindle, didn't matter. The most important thing was that he was alive, amidst family and friends who supported him. He saw how precious life was and the need to enjoy it to the max everyday, every minute, every second.

You see, in effect every one of us is George Bailey and each of us holds the power to positively change bad situations and make them tolerable and better. Sometimes we can't change the outcomes, but we can certainly try and in doing so, ultimately make the world a better place than it was when we were just sitting back idly. Don't get me wrong...such a task can be frustrating, sometimes seeming almost undoable. But it is the attempt that truly makes the difference, showing yourself and others that you didn't let the problem beat you without putting up a good fight. Sue and I approached our lives in this manner. We tried under great burdens to change our lot in life by educating ourselves about cancer, by helping others face their own fight with the disease and by promoting awareness of the plight of cancer survivors.

Sue was George Bailey, giving, caring and loving. She touched so many people's lives by simply being herself. Friends and family are in awe of her courage, bravery, and her strength. Through her teacher career, her involvement in our local school district, her undying spirit encouraging others to fight on, her never give up, never surrender attitude online with the Amazons, or in person with people she met, Sue remained a tower of strength.

Now, don't get me wrong, like George Bailey, she had her moments of despair, anguish, and bitterness. We had gone through the "why me" stage, and the "aren't I a good person so why did I deserve this" phase. There were even thoughts of ending it all when the pain and suffering became unbearable at times as George Bailey felt that Christmas Eve in Bedford Falls when he stood at the edge of the bridge ready to jump into the freezing water below. But through it all, Sue persevered and influenced so many with support, and loving care. As I've said many times in this book, we are not religious people at all, but it gets you to think about a Supreme Being dishing out pain and suffering only to people that can handle it (I wish He/She would have asked Sue and me first!) Apparently, He/She felt that Sue could cope and deal with cancer. Well, He/She got a bonus because Sue did more than just cope, she became a disciple, a courtier, a leader in the fight to make the plight of Stage Four survivors as public as possible, and to help them with advice to live the best life possible under horrific circumstances. Yes, I would say she morphed into the role of guardian angel, a.k.a. Clarence Odbody.

ℒℒℒ

By the way, two asides about the movie…I had a personal love of Clarence, the angel, because he was a dead ringer for my dad. Especially the scene where George is so flustered at the cemetery and he pushes Clarence down to the ground on the bed of snow. Clarence wearing a fedora looks up at George and says to him that life was different because he was never born. Freeze frame that moment as Clarence is looking upward and you will see my dad. A lot of places evoke tears in this movie, but that scene gets me every time!

Matthew applied to Princeton University prior to his eventual acceptance into the school and he had to write an essay about whom you would want (fact or fictional) to change lives with if you could. Matt chose, of course, George Bailey. It was a great essay that captured the essence of what Matthew is all about, a caring, loving soul, who would give you the shirt off his back to help you. Here is some of what he wrote:

> *If I were asked who I believe is the embodiment of good character, I would respond, "George Bailey from the movie* It's a Wonderful Life." *Throughout his life, George tries to leave his little town of Bedford Falls so that he can do something magnificent; he wants to build skyscrapers ten stories high and travel around the world fulfilling his childhood dream;*

yet every time that he tries to leave, he gets drawn back. He knows that if he goes, then his Building and Loan business will fall into the hands of the mean old miser, Mr. Potter. Throughout the movie, George gives of himself and never asks for anything in return. He is thoughtful and modest; the two traits that I believe comprise good character.

Matthew goes on to give examples of how he fits these qualities. He was accepted into Princeton University and the rest was history (actually math!). Thank you Frank Capra and the cast and crew of *It's a Wonderful Life*.

I guess you can save a rental fee at your local video store. If you were not familiar with these three great flicks prior to this chapter, you certainly know them now! There was a lot to internalize from good movies, and Sue and I were fortunate to come across these comedic, powerful, character and strength-building classics.

God Forbid

s you can see, Sue's cancer became more widespread, yet still under control (that sounds like an oxymoron). It became important that a very unclear future should be made clear. Even though the subject of death was taboo, it was necessary to prepare for any possible scenario. I remember back when I was a kid living at home with my parents, such thoughts were never spoken. Never! Mind you, Sue and I were not thinking in terms of impending doom for her, but we knew that we were going to die one day, so why not make it easier for the family members that remain. Cancer has that ugly way of making you think of things that you just can't and don't want to fathom. Not that Sue and I had great amounts of wealth. We did own a house, had two cars, and two very smart children that would someday attend Ivy League Schools, so transferring our minimal assets at the appropriate time (I still have trouble saying "death") to Matt and Justin made lots of sense.

We asked a few friends about lawyers that handle such things as Living Wills and Health Proxies. Sue and I eventually settled on a nice, seemingly competent, female lawyer in a town nearby. We were instructed by her secretary to bring certain documents and important papers, as well as a very large check! All parties sat down in an office the size of Yankee Stadium: plush carpets, a desk made from imported European wood, and beautiful works of art hung on each wall.

At our initial meeting, the lawyer began by asking us pertinent questions about our story, the cancer, the kind of life we led, and our kids. All the while, she was scribbling notes for herself on her legal-sized pad. I actually noticed that in her eyes there appeared to be some moisture, especially when Sue and I discussed our lives with cancer. As it turned out, she shared with us that she had lost her mom to breast cancer as well, so we were obviously hitting a nerve in her. We ended the session, and she had all the information she needed to draw up the papers.

Two weeks passed until our next and final meeting with the lawyer. She started to explain some of the verbiage in the document. When she got to the line that mentioned "in case of death," her eyes departed from the paper, she looked up at us in a very sincere manner and she improvised a "God forbid." Since there were a lot of phrases in the Living Will that talked about death, Sue and I were in for it—God forbid, God forbid, God forbid. She didn't miss a single one. It became comical. Sue and I decided that we had had just about enough, so we winked at each other, planning our next calculated and choreographed move. As she read from the Will, and it came to the death statement, Sue and I got up from our chairs, and led the lawyer and the witness in the room to stand up, waved our arms in a rhythmic motion so that we could all say, "God forbid." It got to the point where I finally had had enough and said, "Look, we all understand by now that God has heard us, and he will show us mercy, especially after having to endure all of these "God forbids" today, so maybe we can dispense with the phrase from here on out, what do you think?"

We all had a good laugh over the whole thing and got through the rest of the day with maybe just a couple of slips on the lawyer's part. Just habit, I guess! All in all, Sue and I counted fifty-eight "God forbids" that day, give or take a few. We had never forbidden anyone from doing anything that many times in the course of three hours!

We actually did the smart thing to set up Wills while we were still alive. It certainly makes the future more acceptable, understandable, and palatable for surviving family members. It will even reduce the guilt that remaining members of the family might have had. There will be no choices for them to make whether or not to resuscitate the patient, or keep them existing (notice I don't say "alive") using various drugs, thus eliminating guilt—"did we do the right thing?" Even though our lawyer had her moments with our case, she did turn out to be very caring, and empathic with our situation. I would certainly recommend this action whether you have health problems or not.

Be Aware of Flying Objects or Hammer Time

After many years of marriage, it becomes obvious that jobs or tasks around the house become designated to a particular member of the family unit. I'll give you an example of what I'm talking about. In our Long Island town, garbage pick-up occurred three times a week: Tuesday, Thursday, and Saturday. It was uncanny, but every time I left the garbage pails filled and prepped for curbside dumping, something always happened with Sue at the helm. Tuesday came and went and the garbage cans were still filled to capacity and in the same place they were on Monday night. Sue's response to this was that she forgot—every time. This reminded me of the very famous Steve Martin comedy routine about getting out of paying your taxes...just say two little words that will save you time and time again—"I Forgot!" Okay, it could happen to anyone. No problem, leave it until Thursday.

Now between Tuesday and Thursday, we accumulated tons more trash (we used to get lots of junk mail). So the garbage receptacles were now overflowing with bagged goodies just waiting to be carted away. Even though our trash cans had wheels under them, somehow with Sue in charge rolling the cans down the driveway to the curb was equivalent to Sir Edmund Hillary forging his way up to the crest of Mount Everest in the Himalayas! The cans somehow tipped over during Sue's wheeling down procedure, and fifteen Hefty trash bags started rolling down our driveway, onto the walkway, and into the street. Sue called for me to come outside and help. Both of us recouped the containers, appropriately placed them in the plastic wheeled cans and got them to the curb just as the garbage truck came barreling down the street with the Sanitation Engineers ready to do some heavy lifting and dumping.

It was apparent by Saturday's pickup that this task had now become mine and only mine. You know the expression, "if you can't take the heat, get out of the kitchen!" Well, if Sue couldn't roll out the garbage, she had to get out of the driveway! Now it wasn't that Sue couldn't perform this job, she just chose a way to get out of doing it—it's called educated incompetence! Show your partner how badly you do a task, and they'll no longer ask you to do it! Bravo, Sue!

Being the quick learner that I profess to be, I pulled a similar stunt to get out of my appointed mission…doing the laundry. Since the onus was on me to do the wash, I made sure to break every rule of "laundry-hood" that I could think of. Whites in with colors, towels in with delicate fabrics, bleach on everything no matter what color it was (very non-discriminatory!), and of course, put too much detergent in the top loader. After my first disastrous attempt at this, it was clear that laundry and I were like an oil spot and water. I got my point across with minimal damages. Yes, I lost a couple nice solid-colored shirts that now resembled the tie-dyed garb that was popular in the 60s. And yes, I lost a couple of hours cleaning up the laundry room from an abundance of suds oozing from the washer down its metallic side and creeping forward on the tiled floor. But it was all in the cause of educated incompetence. My objective was accomplished, and from that moment on, Sue did all of the laundry.

I mentioned these sly maneuvers to weasel out of chores that neither Sue nor I appreciated doing. There was one endeavor that caused both of us to look in the other direction, which was window washing. We had extended our home back sixteen feet, thus adding on seventeen new windows. Those, along with the existing fourteen panes of glass, made window cleaning a real pain! I think that Sue and I took the attitude that nature would tidy up the glass especially after a nice, hard rainstorm left them unsmudged, unsoiled, and squeaky clean, allowing the brilliant sun to shine on through. No Windex needed in this household! When it came to keeping windows neat and fresh, it was crystal clear to us that this laissez-faire policy that Sue and I adopted just wasn't coming clean. It was a transparent attempt to avoid work. For some reason, it just didn't seem to bother us.

Well, twice I wish that our windows were not that "clean." Obviously, they really weren't that sparkling to begin with, but apparently two birds, one in front of the house, and one in the back must have thought that the panes were so immaculate that they weren't even there. That was a total mystery to Sue and me considering the state of our windows. On two different occasions, what must have been two near-sighted birds, decided to fly through seemingly pristine apertures only to crash into closed windows, cracking the panes in half! Please, those of you readers who subscribe to the National Aviary Society of America, don't get angry at Sue and me. We have as much respect for nature through the appreciation of birds as the next person. Trust me, these were two misguided birds (what do you expect, they were bird-brains) who should have noticed our dirty, dusty, non-Windexed, semi-clean windows. They didn't, and unfortunately, the birds and Sue and I paid a costly price. As I said before, what a pain/pane these episodes turned out to be!

I talked earlier in the chapter entitled, "Typhoid" Susan about my propensity to procrastinate. It was a good and lucky thing to bide my time then, but sometimes it can backfire on you. Case in point: the winter was rapidly approaching and certain chores were normally accomplished by that time in the year. One, however, was an accident waiting to happen. The summer patio furniture, heavy wrought iron table with four matching chairs, lay dormant on the concrete patio in our backyard adjacent to the house. Under regular conditions, these items were to be put to sleep for the winter in our garage, protecting them from the blustery elements of Jack Frost. But you know how it is, one thing leads to another, time elapses, and the next thing you realize is that you're way behind schedule. Now I'm not using Sue's cancer as an excuse, but I'm sure that it was a deterrent, plus there was the fact that the patio furniture weighed a ton and the garage wasn't cleared out ready to accept its new tenant for the winter season. So that was the scenario, scene set for the unexpected to happen!

I mentioned the new extension. Its design included four beautiful skylights slightly above eye level when sitting in the kitchen area on the second floor of the house. The dinner table was situated so that two members of the family were facing the skylights and two had their backs to them. Sue and I sat with our backs to the windows and Matthew and Justin sat looking towards the skylights.

We were all eating our supper, talking about the day and what interesting events occurred at school. The television was on softly and the weatherman talked of some really bad weather coming our way…high winds, freezing rain, cold and raw. Wouldn't you know it, almost as if on cue from a movie director, a great gust of wind develops outside. The house shivered from its effects. Suddenly, we all heard a crash downstairs in the den area. Then one of the kids (I can't remember which one) raised his arm and pointed to the skylights, saying, "Hey, that looks like the patio table!" It was like *The Wizard of Oz*! We were back in Kansas and none of us ever clicked our heels. Sue didn't even own a pair of red shoes!

To our amazement, the "two ton" table was swept up, up, and away, reaching our second floor, twisting and turning in flight, then coming down to earth again in our grassy backyard. On the way up, it did some heavy-duty damage to one of the afore-mentioned new windows, cracking it in bits and pieces. This was an unbelievable show of strength and fury on the part of Mother Nature. In retrospect, we were very lucky to have this mammoth of a table do minimal damage to the house. I certainly learned my lesson from this flying episode. Naturally, I got rid of all the outside furniture, never to entertain family and guests alfresco again (only kidding)! I made sure in future years to place the outdoor furniture where it belongs…indoors!

♋♋♋

Continuing in the flying theme, Sue and I never saw someone fly down a ladder as fast as this gentleman in this next vignette. When we moved into our house back in the late 1970s, it was the house we had always dreamed of owning. Remember, we came from a humble abode in Brooklyn to a "mansion" in Long Island. It didn't have everything that we desired, but we knew, in time, Sue and I would transform it into our castle. It came complete with in-wall air conditioners and everything, unlike our first apartment!

The only problem was that the air conditioners were old and in desperate need of a modern, efficient working replacement model. The present air conditioning was installed low down on the wall. Now everyone knows that cold air falls and hot air rises (what keeps me planted with my feet on the ground is beyond me). So, Sue and I figure that since we are buying a new unit, the installer, for a few extra bucks could just patch up the old hole after taking the worn out unit from the wall and make a new hole in the wall, much higher than the previous one to further aid the new AC's efficiency. After some bickering, the contractor agreed to "keep the customer happy." Sue was never good at bartering or negotiating so that very unpleasant task was left for me to accomplish. I must admit, I got better at it the more practice I had doing it.

The next morning, bright and early, the carpenter came to the house, extension ladder, tools and all, along with our brand new AC unit. Pulling the old box from the wall was easy. It was barely hanging on by a thread anyway. Now it was time to determine where to place the new cooler. He zeroed in on a spot about two feet from the ceiling line. Stepping up to the appropriate rung on the ladder, he unholstered his Sawzall, a reciprocating saw that could rip though plywood and two-by-four beams. Mind you, he was now two stories high perched on his ladder, leaning against the side of the house. He mentioned that the wall seems warm but continued to buzz away with his cutting tool. He broke through the first of four cuts for the new aperture. Second side and third side done, cleanly cut, looking good. At this time, something seemed to be vibrating coming from within the wall, but Sue and I thought it was just the Sawzall doing its work.

Suddenly, we heard a crashing sound, a yelping, and a desperate call for help. Sue and I raced outside to witness the man literally jumping off the ladder from a great height, his arms flailing in no apparent pattern, and surrounding his head, with a black cloud, was a swarm of what seemed to be carpenter bees. (you could tell that they were carpenter bees...they all wore tool belts around one of their three waists!). That buzzing sound and that generated heat was the agitation of these bees. The carpenter was disrupting his namesake carpenter bees' home, their peaceful hive nesting inside our walls! Sue and I "sawz it all" and truly, we couldn't believe what we were seeing. We never saw someone run that fast, zig-zagging down the street, trying desperately to evade the invaders. All I could think of was the Beatles song, "Let It *Bee!*" Luckily, the bugs called off the attack, and our carpenter was out of harm's way. Sue and I felt terrible, but we had no way of knowing that our walls were breeding grounds for flying, stinging insects. As the bees put the bite on him, he did the same to us. We compensated our guy very well for all of the trouble he encountered that day.

♒♒♒

A quick story about our Brooklyn place. When Sue and I were first married, we rented this cozy little lovely "penthouse," perfect for two young kids just starting out in life together.

It was a two family house in the heart of Brooklyn's "little" Italy...made mom very proud! Sue did so many decorative things to our little love-nest from sewing cute curtains for the windows to hanging wallpaper. We made it into our "home sweet home." Remember, it was the 70s so we had lots of "apartment life" accoutrements like a brown painted arrow with yellow decal lettering saying "Welcome" leading down the stairs to our front door, and a planter constructed from a six-pack of empty Coca Cola cans each filled with soil with wandering jew foliage and hanging by a row of pop-tops intertwined together. We got those two era-appropriate ideas from reading decorating magazines, so don't laugh too hard at us! From Sue's dad, we obtained a printer's drawer, something very popular in those days. These were actual drawers that were constructed to hold small wooden blocks of different sized fonts to be used in printing. The type-setter would painstakingly pick the letter and font from the tiny compartments within the drawers to be utilized for page layouts. Sue and I had other ideas for its potential. We used to fit little mementos and chachkas that we purchased from our trips and ventures into the miniscule wood-slat cells. But it wasn't enough for us to have your run of the mill printer's drawer...no, not us. With Sue's grudging support, I took off the plywood backing, replaced it with a translucent piece of plastic, stapled a set of Christmas white lights in behind and *oui ala*...we had the only back-lit drawer in existence. Wow! Real 70s stuff, eh?

Okay, the lighted drawer was my crazy idea, and in

retrospect, we probably could have done without it. Sue, however, had great ideas because for the time, her ideas translated into attractive, yet inexpensive adornments for the house. I built a wall-to-wall unit in our living room that became home to our color television, as well as a drawer for papers and a section for wine bottles (made from clay drainage hexagonal cylinders…a world wide search for those, may I add). The unit was designed by Sue and me to center a Castro Convertible pull-out table with leaves and legs to seat and dine eight to ten people. It was functional and decorative as well, and we produced it.

Now the rooms would get a bit stuffy because even though each room had windows, there was just no cross ventilation in the apartment. Sue and I got hold of a very old air conditioner, one that was on its last legs at best. I never liked to see wires hanging or dangling or dragging over floors or carpet. I was a "concealer", a hider of such things. We placed the AC in the front window figuring that it would cool off the living room as well as some of the rest of the four room dwelling. Unfortunately, the outlet located under the window was chock-full of plugs from lamps, clocks and telephones. So I went into action. The first outlet available was one situated in our bedroom. I went to the nearest hardware store and purchased a hundred foot extension cord and feverishly ran it under the newly purchased wall-to-wall rugs, tucking it beneath everything in sight so it wouldn't be visible.

One very hot summer day, Sue was folding laundry in our bedroom. The antiquated air conditioner was pumping out room temperature air at best, really not accomplishing its function but working ever so hard. It didn't matter. Just the sound of an air conditioner churning away was enough power of suggestion for Sue and me to think cool! She started to hear a crackling sound, apparently coming from near or right below her feet. Sue asked me if I heard the sound as well. It was as if someone was stepping on potato chip crumbs. Coincidently, it just so happens that the night before, Sue and I were having a late night snack of Wise Potato Chips in bed so naturally, I dismissed the noise because Sue was stepping on and crunching brittle chip morsels. But now, Sue noticed that the area was starting to feel a bit heated, and then smell of an ashy-burning. To both our surprise, a hole of burnt carpet fibers now appeared on the bedroom floor. It was the covered wire under the carpet in the bedroom leading from the living room AC that had started to smolder. We quickly shut off the AC, unplugged the extension cord, and poured water on the rug to dowse any potential future embers. I certainly learned a lesson that day...never conceal live wires under anything—especially carpets—and always use the correct gauge wire for air conditioners...LAMP CORD quality won't cut it! At the young, tender age of twenty-four, I was unaware that there were different capacities of wires for specific jobs around the house. But mainly, I brutally learned not to dabble in fields (of electricity) that are foreign to you. Leave certain things, like electricity, to those that have been around the "circuit" and to those that stay "current" in such matters! Seriously though, my stupidity and inattentiveness could have cost us our lives and I never forgot that experience.

☙☙☙

The final segment of this chapter is needed to set straight a Shangri-la existence between Sue and me that has been painted for you, the reader. I talk about an idyllic picture of our marriage, and it was. But believe it or not, Sue and I do not belong on the top of the wedding cake replacing those two perfect bride and groom figurines blissfully holding hands. Earlier in the book I mentioned that our taste in music was drastically different. That was one small difference of opinion, but that's nothing. We did have our moments just like any couple. One that comes to mind goes under the category of "Hammer Time."

Sue and I moved into this great house on Long Island, but as I mentioned before, it didn't have everything that we wanted in a home. It was lacking a fireplace, a big, beautiful bow window in the living room facing a pink flowering Chinese Maple tree that bloomed for two weeks a year in the spring (for the next two weeks, it left us pink snow), and just that certain something that makes a house become a home. We took care of the fireplace and bow window, but Sue and I decided to transform our plain, stark looking bedroom into a dreamy, romantic space where we could both be swept away by its beauty and uniqueness. This was all Sue needed to hear, and she went into action. She ran down to the corner newsstand and picked up a bunch of home designing magazines. Hey, it worked for our Brooklyn 70s pad, so why not now?

Sue was terrific at seeing something in a magazine, form-fitting the idea to our situation, then blue-printing the plan out on graph paper (see…applying math again into our lives for practical purposes). The rest was up to me to transfer the ink on the paper into real wooden beams, screws, and nails. We worked very well together as a team. When I needed help holding lumber straight or needed an accurate measurement on some calculation or just simply needed to be handed a tool, Sue was there. Now while I was building a new wall-to-wall closet complete with sliding doors and a full length mirror on rollers attached to one of them, Sue was sewing curtains for the wall on the left and right side of the bed. The coup-de-grâce was a gorgeous fabric canopy that Sue tailored out of the same curtain material. It hovered over the headboard and spanned about a third of the length of the bed.

Everything was going along swimmingly until I reached a snag in production. The mirror part of the sliding door was not coming out the way we had envisioned it. I thought that the mirror was too bare standing alone and it required a border of some kind. Sue suggested placing the mirror on a piece of plywood that framed the glass by three inches on its sides. Then we should purchase a plastic pool hose and cut it in half so that it was now shaped like semi-circular tubes. At this point, I was looking at her like, "Have you lost your mind? Pool hose adjacent to a mirror? What?" She continued her thought…glue the semi-circular tubes to the plywood, then glue some of the extra left-over fabric from the canopy on to the tubes. You now have a beautiful border surrounding what will appear to be a built in mirror. Brilliant, eh?

After her well-meaning, well thought out ten minute dissertation, I laughed at the very thought of it. My reaction to her idea provoked Sue to do something I never would have expected. She picked up the very hammer that she had been graciously handing to me when I was in need of it, and flung it at me and my stinking mirror! It was like watching the action in slow motion…the hammer rotating through the air like a discus throw at the Olympics, getting ever so near to its intended targets, and making that sound when an object cuts through the wind. Now Sue was not a sports participant (read back earlier about our first date attending a hockey game); lucky for me and the glass. The hammer kind of died in flight just before the bull's-eye. Sue stormed out of the room, and I was left speechless and totally sorry for hurting her. Of course my proud male ego didn't allow me to run after her, hug her, and apologize for my insensitivity.

We obviously did patch things up between us. It went something like this: one of us said, "I'm sorry" and the other one said, "It's okay Joe!" Other skirmishes Sue and I had, infrequent as they were, ended usually in the same dialogue as well! I will say this, however. After Sue's cancer diagnosis in 1992, we rarely disagreed about much of anything. You see, we had a common enemy to fight and argue with. The disease really put things into perspective about what was truly important in life. If it was possible, we actually loved each other even more than before, and life's little bumps in the road remained just that...trivial and unimportant.

Post Script to the hammer throw saga...I can not tell you how many people complimented Sue and me on this rolling mirror with the border of hidden pool hoses and fabric. Yes, I followed Sue's idea to a tee and it did come out great. Why didn't I do that in the first place?

So, please be aware of flying objects of all kinds...tables, hammers, and of course, the birds and the bees!

Introducing Spinal Tap— It Rocked Our World

In 2001, Sue and I experienced the first of four spinal taps—also referred to as lumbar punctures—that she was to have done. Being Stage Four, there are so many places the cancer could go. Vagueness about where it was hiding in the body was great. Whenever there was some change in Sue, whether it was Bell's Palsy, tingling sensations, numbness, or a rise in the CA 27/29 cancer blood test markers, it was of utmost importance to check her spinal fluid. Similarly, when Sue's cancer metastasized to her bones, it was vital to check that it hadn't gone further, namely into the liver. This was particularly frightening when we first sat down with the neurologist, who was very concerned about Sue's droopy, right side of her face. He had read the earlier reports which seemed to indicate that cancer was not the cause of the Palsy, rather it was a virus pressing on the facial nerves. Sue was on chemotherapy which, when working its magic to kill the cancerous cells, also lowers the body's resistance to other bacterial or viral infections. That was the thought process going into this appointment with the neurologist.

We sat on the other side of his desk, which had on it plastic models of the brain, the spinal cord, and the skull. The spinal fluid which flows up and down the spine also bathes the brain. This liquid, because of its proximity to very vital organs, becomes so important in the life and death struggle of a cancer patient. All it takes is a single cancerous cell to find its way into the spinal fluid, and thus the brain, spine, and all of the body parts that those two organs control, namely virtually everything neurological, would be at the mercy of the disease.

This particular doctor was not one for pulling punches; rather he was straight up and in your face with the facts. His approach was very different from our oncologist, who was more laid back and soft-spoken. We were shocked to hear him say that if cancer ever reached the spinal fluid, the patient would have on an average of three to six months to live. You could just imagine the sinking feeling, the hopelessness of the situation when it was time to schedule a tap.

The day arrived and Sue and I went to the hospital where the neurologist was affiliated. We were terrified. Not only had we never experienced one of these procedures, but the wait for the results would be excruciating. Sue left me to get her hospital gown on, opened in the back so the doctor had access to the spine. I asked if I could come in as well, and he granted me my request. I stood in front of Sue; the doctor was at her back. The nurse applied the orange-ish antiseptic and a numbing agent on Sue's back. The doctor waited a minute or two while the anesthesia took full effect. With Sue sitting at the edge of the table, he then asked her to to lean forward into my stomach and chest, arching her back in a convex position, the idea being that this would separate the spinal disks enough to get a needle in between two of them. He inserted the needle, and Sue let out a piercing scream that must have shaken the walls. The first attempt to draw fluid failed. He repeated it two more times until finally the fluid oozed out to fill up two test tube vials. The procedure was done. Now we just had to wait.

We got home and, suddenly, Sue felt this tremendous pressure in her head when in an upright position. I immediately called the doctor to find out what could be happening. The secretary informed us that Sue was experiencing a spinal tap headache. The pain Sue was feeling was so great that that was all she could think of. I really believed that, at that very moment, the results of the procedure—which would be life or death answers—didn't matter! She needed to get rid of this tremendous throbbing in her head. The instructions were for Sue to lay on her side for at least two or three days, and that she drink fluids that contained electrolytes to replenish the lost spinal fluid. Sue's headache ended up lasting four days, and it was on the fourth day that we received the results that the tap was clean. That was a great relief mentally, but now we still needed to work on the physical side. This episode was one of the lower points for us throughout this entire ordeal. There was a feeling that the results could spell the end of our run together, a team formed from heaven, now being dismantled, cell by cell, fluid by fluid, organ by organ. We both knew the severity of the situation was extreme if any doctor was thinking that a spinal tap was necessary.

Sue went on to have three more of these taps but it wasn't until the third one that we found a neurologist that could perform these in his own office using a very special instrument. He, too, used the needle to do the tap, but his needle was slightly different. The best way I could describe it was that it was a needle in a needle. He pierced Sue's skin with the outer needle, but it was the inner one that drew the fluid out. The cost for the use of this paraphernalia was an extra $10 above our co-pay, but it was worth every penny. Going home in the car after the tap, Sue was lying on the back seat down flat on her side. I pulled up to our house, not sure what to expect. She started to rise from her supine position very slowly and carefully. We needed to get her up the stairs and on the living room couch without much jostling. She sat up expecting the pain, but nothing. She got out of the car tentatively…still no pain, no pressure. Amazing! The third neurologist was absolutely correct—the miracle needle avoided the tap headache. Sue was able to function on her feet as if nothing had been done at all.

One last issue that came with each tap—the hope that the puncture hole in the lumbar made by the needle would stop oozing fluid and eventually clot itself to closure. What if that didn't happen? What if the wound continued to spew bodily fluids? The way that this is usually handled post-procedure is by taking some of the patient's blood and placing it over the puncture hole. Once the blood was exposed to the air, it coagulated, closing the pin prick and eventually stopping the flow of fluids. This was all well and good for most people. You see, there was always a question whether Sue's blood was tainted with cancer cells, though. If that were to be the case, by placing her flawed blood next to the open area leading to the spinal fluid, the doctor may well have been introducing the cancer cells to an otherwise clean and clear fluid! This was truly a question that had the experts reeling. The oncologist and neurologists conference-called about this very query and they never came up with an acceptable answer. Many of the decisions (which protocol to follow, what medical test to use, and so on) made by the doctors were based on results from previous studies or test cases. Not a single one had ever heard of such a potential problem from previous test trials, and one of the neurologists honestly told us that he had never even thought about the chance of this happening. Sue actually had brought up a truly interesting, thought-provoking question. It was never resolved, but thankfully, in Sue's case it was never an issue. To the doctors' credit, they didn't just slough it off as unimportant, but rather they did their best to find answers to solve the issue. Doctors—and I mean good ones who aren't high and mighty but instead willing to listen and maybe even learn a thing or two from their patients—were the types of professionals that Sue and I associated with. Thank goodness for that!

The New Millennium

When one is diagnosed with breast cancer, it is human nature to think that it is a death sentence. Yes people do beat the odds, but will I be in that crowd? I must admit, Sue reaching the year 2000 was a dream at one point, especially when the cancer resurfaced in 1998. Of course, neither of us ever expressed those sentiments to each other, but living with the burden of cancer day in and day out, the blessing of another day brought on hope that we too would be in that elite group of cancer-beaters.

Living with Stage Four cancer is like toiling around with an elephant on your back. You become used to the weight after a while, but you know the tonnage is there. You don't want the elephant to get larger because, eventually, the weight will break your back. So you try not to feed it, feed into fears of what could happen. Sue was great at not succumbing to the thoughts and anxieties of Stage Four. She did have her moments, but supporting members, be it family, friends, or Amazons, were there to set her straight once again. So the date—January 1, 2000—almost became a goal, an ambition, a destination at which to arrive. Not looked upon as an end, just a point to springboard from.

Remember back to the time of the millennium, computers were going to crash from the fact that 00 (the last two numbers of the year 2000) doesn't follow the number 99 (from 1999) chronologically? Companies were scrambling, financial institutions were panicking that all computerized records would be lost, religious followers were calling for the apocalypse, and the world was ready to celebrate. One thing Sue and I found cool was the networks had coverage of every time zone as the clock struck twelve. At six in the morning on New Year's Eve day, we watched television and chuckled when we saw a couple of isolated aborigines around a campfire in the white sand celebrating the New Year in the tiny remote island of Tonga, just west of the International Date Line, thinking that in eighteen hours, these three Tongans would be lost in a sea of humanity if they were located in Times Square! They were probably asked to dance around at the stroke of twelve in exchange for humpback whale blubber by the one cameraman that lost his office pool; assignment Tonga…go cover it for New Years Eve! There was something to be said however about the serene, peaceful image of that island setting. What encouraged Sue and me was that at twelve midnight Tongan time, the ground they were standing on didn't suddenly open up into a giant fissure in the soil, swallowing everyone (all three aborigines) up in its path. Rule out the apocalypse! As midnight swept across the globe, every major city and country was featured: Sydney, Australia; Tokyo, Japan; Beijing, China; New Delhi, India; Moscow, Russia; London, England; and so on. It was interesting to see the divergent worldwide celebrations, traditional to the country and area. It was also nice and comforting to see, with each passing hour, the world was still the world.

Sue and I hosted our gala New Year's Eve party, with my brother and his family, my parents, and other friends huddled together, laughing, drinking, and eating because all was right, the globe didn't disintegrate, our piddly amount of money was safe, our family was together, and most importantly Sue's new protocol was working to keep the cancer at bay. We were in a partying mood and party we did. We partied like it was 1999! We all had a great time conversing, playing pool and ping-pong, singing, and even dancing. The television was on, a din in the background until around 11:45 p.m. We all sat watching intently as New Yorkers prepared for the New Year to greet us. Maybe in the recesses of our minds, there might have been a thought that something *evil* might occur in New York, the happening place to be, the financial capital of the world. As the countdown began—ten, nine, eight seconds left—I nestled up to Sue holding her tight. Four, three, two, one…Happy New Year! The kids were popping Silly String all over the house and us—we kissed like we never kissed before, thankful that she and I were *both* able to see today happen, and hopeful that there would be many more New Year's Eve celebrations.

Everyone was so festive, the champagne was flowing, life was good, and everyone hugged and kissed everyone else in the room. Then, suddenly, at 12:05 a.m., the television screen turned into static. It caught everyone's attention. For a good thirty seconds, the sound on the television filled the room and people started to get a little edgy. The static dissipated to reveal a strange, yet familiar image—a picture of none other than Dr. Evil from the movie, *Austin Powers*. He began to speak…

This is Dr. Evil, also known as your "Millennium Madman." Don't try to change the channel or adjust your vertical. I have taken over. Not even a BILLION dollars will change my mind…well maybe a billion. Scott, is this the best picture you could find of me? Here are my demands as your new ruler:

1. *Time magazine will name me "Madman of the Century."*
2. *You will all be strapped down to a chair and forced to watch Regis and Kathy Lee.*
3. *Richard Simmons must have a diet of Kentucky Fried Chicken for the rest of his life.*
4. *Baywatch reruns will air on television, throughout the day, on all channels (including cable).*
5. *MOST IMPORTANT…Ex-President Bill Clinton will give me the names and phone numbers of all of his presidential interns.*

Have a wonderful Millennium. Good Bye! Ha, ha, ha, ha, ha….

At 11:50 p.m., I had positioned the VCR controls next to me on the couch. After all of us had a chance to wish each other a "Happy New Year," the time was ripe for me to push the play button. I wasn't going to let this momentous occasion happen without doing something people would remember it by. No one, not even my own family, had suspected anything like this, especially from a technically challenged person such as myself. Confusion at first transformed quickly into laughter as the tape played on. The guests all turned to me for some kind of explanation. I fessed up—yea, it was me. All right, so I'm not a comedy writer, but the intentions were good!

♋♋♋

As it turned out, the beginning years of new millennium were a continuation of the old millennium with regards to Sue and her health status. We were in a fairly good position. The drugs that Sue was taking caused her little to no side effects, and they appeared to be working. She did experience some lower back pain that would shoot straight down her leg. Our home remedy was over the counter pain medicines and hot water. We had installed three body sprays in the shower in the master bathroom and a seat in the corner of the wall opposite those nozzles. The water shot out of the pressurized heads, and we directed the pulsating stream onto Sue's back and leg. What a difference it made to her. The combination of the meds, the hot water, and my massages seemed to help to alleviate the pain. Yes, we were like the boy with his finger in the dyke—the cancer was being held at bay, no "flood" of problems, and things were actually improving. There had been no evidence of new disease and recent blood tests were indicating that the tumor markers were trending downward, exactly what Sue and I needed to see.

Questions, however, always pervaded our minds. How long of a positive run could we get on the protocol set out for us by the oncologist? Sue was always very lucky that she would not only be able to handle the side effects of her drugs, but she also got great use out of them way beyond the average time of supposed effectiveness. This is what a Stage Four survivor needed to have happen because the more time one drug is effectively working, the more drugs you'll have still in the arsenal to fall back on and try when the present drug finally loses its ability to stave off the cancer which unfortunately will happen as the cancer "learns" to adapt to the old drug. When and if the cancer reared its ugly head again, where would it attack next? Would we be able to find meds that would fight it off one more time? Would Sue be able to tolerate them? You can see that at Stage Four, you have many more questions than you have answers. Questions gave way to a shaky confidence that all was going to be okay. But just as we had survived the projected troubles that the millennium was to have brought on and didn't, Sue and I felt that we could survive and thrive for a good long time at Stage Four.

The Final Page
in the Photo Album

Writing this book has been like flipping through the thousands of pages in our family photo album…some pictures make you cry, some make you laugh. Either way, they do conjure up memories. Pictures may fade but memories can never be taken away. After sharing with the you, the reader, all of our lovely pictures over the years, it's now time to turn the page to the final montage of images in the album.

As 2005 began, the number of doctor appointments increased ten-fold. We were battling so many fronts by this time, cancer, Bell's Palsy, numbness, balance, hearing, skin carcinoma, heart issues, and eye difficulties. The least worry for Sue's oncologist was the skin carcinoma, but for some reason, Sue needed to address it. The oncologist kept reassuring her that this was a squamous cell cancer, and in the big scheme of things, it could be left untreated in comparison to the multitude of Sue's other problems.

Despite that, Sue insisted to have it taken care of. We went to a dermatologist who biopsied the spot on her chest. It did turn out to be a squamous cell carcinoma. This is actually the second best type of skin cancer to have, if you have to have any at all. The rarest yet deadliest form is malignant melanoma. This kind of skin cancer tends to spread throughout the body using the lymphatic system as its highway. The most common form is Basal skin melanoma. This is highly treatable and can be cured. Sue's goal was to eradicate the skin cancer using a method called the Mohs micrographic surgery, thus removing the cancer and as little normal tissue as possible. During this surgery, the physician removed a layer of skin and then used a microscope to look at the cancerous area to make sure no cancer cells remained. The procedure took forever because each layer of skin that was removed had to be biopsied to see which layer eventually is cancer free. After each tier was removed, Sue and I went back to the waiting room and stayed until the verdict was given…if cancer, then there was the removal of the next sheet of skin and back to square one. If no cancer, then the procedure was done. Three layers were biopsied before the dermatologist found Sue's skin to be cancer free. I guess, in retrospect, this was Sue taking control of an out-of-control situation. Her life was now being dominated by doctor after doctor planning her life's schedule out for her. Even though this little "non-threatening" cancer was a speck of sand on an already troubled beach, Sue needed to take charge of life and she did.

The bigger issues were trying to find a cause for the Bell's Palsy and a way to deal with its symptoms, and of course, finding a chemo or hormonal drug therapy that would steady and lower the upward trend occurring on the CA 27 / 29 cancer blood test marker numbers. The Bell's Palsy and increase in cancer activity might have been related items. We were in a vicious circle when it came to the Bell's Palsy. Sue's eye couldn't close all the way down, thus exposing her cornea to the wind causing tremendous dryness. Her eyelid was vital in maintaining moisture as well as keeping the eye cleansed. The dryness was also a result of all of the chemotherapy Sue was taking through all of the years. Sue could no longer produce tears. She used saline eye drops that I purchased for her. Each boxful contained individual vials of fluid. She went through those like water! It never seemed like she was able to keep moisture level up fast enough to satisfy her need. After months of dealing the best we could with this problem, we both decided to look into other means of comfort.

We met with an eye surgeon who suggested a couple of ways to treat the problem. One was called tarsorrhaphy, an outpatient surgical procedure where the corners of the eyelids are partially sewn together creating a narrower opening between the upper and lower lids. In doing so, the eyes are exposed to less air and were given a greater opportunity at obtaining moisture and lubrication. The other possibility was surgically implanting a gold weight in the upper eyelid to help the eyelid down. The added weight along with gravity would afford the eye the protection it needed against the elements.

The gold weight as opposed to another type of metal weight was intriguing because of Sue's numerous trips to an MRI machine. Gold would not be affected by the magnetic pull of an MRI. It too was done on an outpatient basis, so it came down to choices: did we or did we not need to put Sue through another procedure? As it turned out, we decided to hold off on any extra surgery for the meanwhile and since we were no longer traveling great distances (other than to doctors) we kept Sue's eye closed with the use of a patch moistened with eye drops.

But through it all, she continued to live a "normal" life usually with a smile on her face (half of it due to the palsy!) and a never say die attitude. It was getting much harder for Sue however to see the positive light at the end of the tunnel. She had her moments with anxiety and depression. Assessing all of her ailments caused her to take a harsh look at reality and she expressed her feelings in an e-mail in August to the Amazons' online board for all to read. It was a piece written about her frustrations, her concerns about her cancer journey but it also offered some hope:

> *To All of My Amazon Friends,*
>
> *Long story made short: I was diagnosed in 1992: had left mastectomy, seven positive lymph nodes. Did nine months of chemo and was "cured" until 1998. Bone mets treated hormonally (mostly Femera and Zoladex). 2001 I got mets to the bone marrow and liver. Taxotere, Herceptin, and Navelbine failed so I went on Xeloda and Lupron and did*

great. The liver mets seem to have subsided although they still show up on the scans-there are no symptoms physically of any liver problems at all.

Throughout this time, I would occasionally have neurologic symptoms. My jaw went numb for a long time, and then I got Bell's Palsy repeatedly. We found a spot in the skull probably causing all this and I had fourteen brain/skull rads last summer. There was no brain mets but the rads treat the whole head. Things improved a great deal, but I'm still not in the normal CA27/29 range. I've been on Doxil and Lupron for sixteen months and aside from the annoying side effects of the Doxil, I feel really good. I still have a wig and now a hearing aid (from the skull mets pressing on the nerve and then the radiation). I've recently had a worsening of the hearing and some fuzziness, so we continue to take MRIs and keep an eye on the situation. So life is not normal but it's better than I could have expected after 12+ years of cancer.

I have two wonderful sons, one starting his first graduate year at Berkeley and one going into his senior year at high school. They were only four and nine when all of this began. It's a miracle we all managed to keep our sanity throughout!! My husband Joe has been a fabulous support to me. It's been really hard on him and he has suffered emotionally for it.

I have days and weeks where I feel depressed and sorry for myself, and other times when I feel almost normal. I am thankful that new meds have allowed me to live a somewhat normal life while going through treatment, but I am frustrated that we are not near a cure. I am angry that people are dying

of cancer and the world is not noticing. They are noticing the
survivors with the pretty pink ribbons. I am scared that we
will run out of treatments and have nothing to turn to.
Susan

In February, seeing that her cancer numbers were steadily increasing, the oncologist ordered a stop to Doxil, Lupron, and Aromasin. From February to the first week of August, Sue experienced a number of side effects from tingling in her arms, frequent headaches, backaches, and ear and jaw pain along with her facial paralysis. Her list of medications looked like the inventory at the local pharmacy. We kept incredible records of medications and times and side effects, but even those pages started to run out of space in the margins. There was one point where Sue was taking six medications at home as well as the chemo prescribed by the various doctors dealing with her case. At home I was administering Ativan, Lexapro, Neurontin, Tylenol, Aleve, and Immodium, in conjunction with Procrit, Gemzar, Zometa, Neupogen, and Faslodex at the oncologist's office.

In mid-August, after the results of CA 27/29 showed that Sue's numbers went up by 73 points to 185.2, it was obvious that a chemotherapy change was necessary. The oncologist who always tried to soften the blow told us these three meds, Velban, Methotrexate, and Thiotepa, when used in tandem, had shown improvement in a study that he read about. He did indicate that other than that one he didn't have any prior studies on these chemos to fall back on.

So basically this was it. All of Sue's and my hopes fell on three drugs, the last three left for us to try. There was no looking back at past drugs. Once they were utilized and lost their effectiveness, we couldn't use them any longer. Sue's last words in her letter to the Amazons was so prophetic: "I am scared that we will run out of treatments and have nothing to turn to." Thirteen years of struggle fell onto the shoulders of Velban, Metatrexate, and Thiotepa. The hope was that we could get a good long run on these meds, so that if and when the time came that they also lost effectiveness, the FDA and the government would have approved of new chemotherapies to use to prolong the fight.

The implementation of these new drugs brought on the requirement of one more test. After years and years of chemo elapses, it took its toll on other organs in the body. The heart, a muscle pumping away, could be harmed by repeated usage of poisonous chemo. Sue needed to take an exam that would test her heart's capabilities to work…the MUGA test. The MUGA scan which stands for Multi-gated Acquisition scan, tests the strength of the heart. All of these drugs are considered potentially "cardiotoxic" because they can damage the heart muscle in some patients, so now everything depended on whether or not Sue's heart could tolerate the new protocol. I knew Sue had enough heart to fight, but would her heart allow it? The procedure was fairly easy so now came the waiting game.

We quickly received the word, via the oncologist the next day, that Sue's heart was functioning at a good enough level to withstand the rigors of the new chemo regimen. The rapidity of the findings of the MUGA test was in itself a clue to the severity of the situation. The oncologist wanted the results quickly so he could start to administer the chemo stat. At that time, Sue never outwardly told me about her fears, but she started to rely upon anti-anxiety medications more than before. She didn't need to say it because I was feeling exactly what she was emotionalizing. The thought pervaded our minds…the end of the thirteen year journey was near.

During August and into September, Sue's ailments escalated instead of subsiding. Her aches (bone pains in her back and leg, frequent headaches, more jaw numbness than before) remained for longer durations of time and much more intense than in the past. We were eventually able to stem the tide and get some problems under control, but it was becoming more of an effort. She needed to take more and more over the counter painkillers than before. Her appetite diminished and her weight was dropping. She seemed to be losing steam, stamina, and strength. You just got the feeling that the cancer was traveling at will, ravaging any and all parts of Sue's body. Mentally, she was Sue, still beating me to the punch at crossword puzzles, still reading books and articles, and still communicating with friends and e-mailing Amazons. Her letters were filled with fear and much less promise of a positive outcome. Sue was facing death head-on, and all I could do was to be there for her. We talked about the concept of an end, of leaving the world a little better place because she was born into it. All the while, I let her talk, expressing her feelings and I held back the tears. She didn't need me blubbering like a baby—she needed to talk. When Sue needed to rest and eventually fell asleep, I went into our bedroom and cried...partly feeling sorry for me, partly feeling sorry for Matthew and Justin, but mainly thinking what a brave, courageous lady Sue was. I was in awe of her—how she was able to openly deal with her situation knowing full well that it seemed to be worsening. Remember back that death was a taboo topic in my parents' household so to hear Sue talk that way was certainly shocking and frightening. We both knew the score...cancer was beating us. Only one of us was willing to accept the facts. What an amazing woman!

She always tried to put on a good face when it came to Justin. Remember, he was going into his senior year at the high school, living at home, and witnessing every emotion that Sue and I expressed. He lived this trek with us, every day for thirteen years. It was hard for him to see his mom's decline. We tried our best to "normalize" life for him...he deserved nothing less. Luckily, Justin had a great bunch of friends that would help to sweep his thoughts away from the morose scenes at home. Still, it was traumatizing for him. The prospects of not having your mom around for such important events in your life—your graduation from high school, the prom, your acceptance to a college, your wedding, the rest of your entire life—certainly was staring Justin square between the eyes. The worst part of this scenario was that Sue and I seemingly could do nothing to change the course. The current against us was rising and becoming harder to navigate, almost like an eddy swirling us any which way it wanted. Here is a snippet of a letter I wrote to an ex-colleague friend of mine from Parkland High School in late August:

> *With Matt away at school for much of Sue's bout with cancer, unfortunately, Jus has seen it all. He has lived it with us, and to his credit, he has been able to overcome the ups and downs of this disease and still flourish at school. It is a testament to his strength and courage. He, too, is quite a kid.*

Matthew was "safely" tucked away in Berkeley beginning his five-year study in mathematics with the eventual end to result in a PhD in that field. Doctor Matt had a nice ring to it, and he immersed himself in his work. That has always been Matthew's modus operandi. But don't get me wrong, he had one eye on his books, but the other was firmly planted on his mom and her condition. We all have our own defense mechanisms. He cared deeply for his mom, as did Justin, but I believed the distance away from home helped to soften the blow somewhat for Matthew. Nevertheless, Sue and I felt so sorry that the kids had to experience this whole episode at all but we carried on as a family as best we could.

In the past, when a new regimen was introduced into Sue's system, the standard span of time to allow the chemo to work on the cancer was three months, at which point, a CA 27/29 blood test was performed. Based on the eroding situation that the oncologist was hearing from us, he asked for Sue to take the blood test weeks earlier than usual so he could determine the effectiveness of the three chemos. There were too many signs heading in the wrong direction to think that the final try was working. Sue was exhibiting nausea, headaches, numbness, and tingling in her hands and jaw, achiness in her legs and joints, tiredness and fatigue and in general, a malaise. Sue's appetite was diminishing rapidly. She said that she had a metallic taste in her mouth, not to mention mouth sores as well. These symptoms could not have been helping her willingness to get nourishment as well.

We went to the oncologist's office as we had done seemingly a thousand times before, but this visit was different. There was no anticipation or anxiety on Sue's face. She was tired of the battle. It was almost like she was ready to hear the negative verdict. She seemed at peace, her body unable to muster up any emotions. We had been down this road before, and we knew what was going to be said to us. I understood her reaction but I refused to give in. I vowed to Sue thirteen years ago that I would fight on to the very last day for her. I wasn't ready to accept the signs flashing all around me. We *will* beat this. My emotions got in the way of acting properly for Sue.

He called us in to the examination room and told us the news we were so sure was coming. Sue's markers continued to climb and there was no other place to turn to. I frantically asked him tons of questions: maybe we need to give the meds more time, maybe the test was inaccurate, maybe, just maybe, there might be another drug to try. I wasn't making any sense in my ranting and raving and Sue sat there, motionless, almost in a trance. She wanted to go home. That was it. She needed to be in the comfort of her own home. The oncologist said we would continue the present protocol because there was nothing left to use, but it was left unsaid that his expectations were not high barring a miracle.

In early September, Sue woke from a sleep to realize that she couldn't move her left arm. We first thought that maybe she slept on it and it required some time to shake itself out of numbness. That was not to be the case. Out of the blue, Sue suddenly couldn't use her arm. I called the oncologist immediately, but he was seeing patients at the time. The secretary informed me that as soon as he could, he would call me back. Hours lapsed and still no phone call. It was torturous, minutes like lifetimes passing us by, endlessly waiting for a phone call while Sue and I struggled to make sense out of this. Why was this happening, what will the doctor say, can't the cancer just leave us alone, hasn't it done enough damage to poor Sue, and of course, why did Sue deserve this lot in life in the first place? Inwardly crying and sobbing, I tried my best to hold it together for her. Sue, on the other hand, was sitting on the couch, staring at the ceiling, stoically calm and tranquil. I don't know what must have been going on in her mind, fear and sadness probably, though she didn't express it, but you got the feeling from her demeanor that she was totally under control and accepting of her situation.

At this point Sue was prone to taking frequent naps so about five o'clock she was in bed resting when the phone rang. Finally, it was the oncologist. He heard about the new symptom and was now prepared to deliver what had to be a very distressing speech. In all the years that Sue and I got to know and "befriend" our doctor, he always referred to Sue and me as Mrs. and Mr., never calling either of us by our first names. I guess dealing with so many patients that don't survive cancer had a way of wearing one down so the impersonal Mrs. and Mr. allowed the doctor to do his job unemotionally by keeping his distance. I picked up the receiver only to hear him say, "Hi, Joe?" Right away, I knew this would be the phone call I wished that we would have never had to receive. He never called me by my first name…why now? He went on to say that, based on the data, all of Sue's recent symptoms and her blood markers rising, it was apparent that the chemos were not working. His exact words to me were that we fought the good fight, but it was time now to make Sue comfortable. He mentioned hospice services for the first time to me. I couldn't believe what he was saying. Actually I could believe it, I just didn't want to hear what he was saying. There was a moment of silence on my end of the conversation. The doctor went on to say how sorry he was that things turned out the way they did and how much he liked us as patients. We were probably one of the younger clients that he dealt with. He expressed the fact that our visits to him were enlightening because, unlike other older patients who sometimes didn't even know the names of the chemo medicines they were using (that generation accepted the doctor's word as gold, never questioning decisions), Sue and I were a breath of fresh air always coming prepared with questions or print outs, for his perusal, studies that we researched involving new drugs that one day could possibly benefit Sue. But now it was time to keep Sue comfortable. Those words resonated in my head bringing back memories of the first day in 1992 when the doctor came into the waiting room at the hospital and he said Sue had cancer.

I thanked the doctor for being there for us for all those years and hung up the phone. I needed time to process what was just told to me, but before I could do that, I ambled downstairs to the den, far enough away from Sue, and I wailed like a baby, tears pouring faster than I could wipe them away. Loud screams of sorrow and grief, uncontrollable moans, and wide range of thoughts. I didn't know what to do. I debated as to whether or not I should share the conversation that had just taken place with Sue. What good would it do if she found out that her doctor had now "given up" on her? I wanted to keep things positive with Sue, so right or wrong, I did not share this information with her. Instead, I looked into hospice care. Hospice is a care service that assists terminally ill patients, usually those who are expected to live less than six months. Although hospice does not provide treatment, it can give comfort, pain relief, and dignity to cancer patients nearing the end of their lives. Sue deserved that kind of care, but accepting these services meant that I too had given up the battle. Logically, I knew it was the right thing to do. After all, doctors are not in the business of losing their patients. They will do everything humanly possible to maintain life, but when the treatments are no longer accomplishing what

254

they were set out to do, it is time to back off. I knew that. I saw it firsthand happening to Sue, but I just couldn't bring myself to admit it, not after fighting, scratching, and clawing for thirteen years. My heart said one thing, my head said the opposite.

I started e-mailing and calling friends over the next few days while Sue was sleeping. Probably the most difficult phone call I had to make was to Matthew. He was at Berkeley for about a month. I did not know the timing, but I certainly wanted Matthew to come home and be with his mother. I was afraid that if he didn't come now, he might have lost an opportunity to say good-bye. He was in disbelief over what I had to say to him. Mind you, Sue and I never sugar-coated the cancer news, but we always managed to put a positive spin on whatever was necessary to relate. This time, there was nothing positive I could say except come home. He listened intently to what I had to reluctantly tell him, and he agreed to trek back to see his mom—maybe for the last time. Telling Justin was just as hard. I don't know how he was able to concentrate on school. He was starting his senior year at the high school, a very important one for him, and now he had to also contend with his mom's demise. I felt so helpless, so sad for the boys. I tried to be there for them, answering any questions, allowing them to vent—anything—but I couldn't replace their mom. Nobody could, and they were feeling the pain.

Since this chapter is about photographs in our album there is a picture I snapped at just the right moment. It shows the love between Matthew, Justin and Sue. She was resting comfortably in our recliner leaning back wearing her favorite robe and a turban to keep her hairless scalp warm, on one arm of the chair was Justin perched with his body facing Sue, and next to him in a folding chair was Matthew, all eyes on one another adoring each other's presence and enjoying the moment. They were chitchatting about nothing important and it didn't matter. They needed to be exactly where they were then, together, maybe for the very last time just soaking in every minute.

Sue continued to weaken physically to the point where her legs could no longer support her disappearing frame. Her body was shutting down but not her mind. We were still able to talk to each other as always. The problem was that she was eating like a bird, picking here and there as she just couldn't stomach something substantial. I rented a wheelchair just so that she was able to be somewhat mobile in the house, but it was becoming increasingly difficult for me to properly care for her needs.

At some point during Matthew's visit, Sue did something that was so emblematic of her and her life. She was lying in our bed, sitting up, and she called Matthew and Justin individually into the room. She spelled out what her hopes and dreams were for them. She told them how proud she was of them and how she knew that they would accomplish anything they set out to in life. She told them how much she loved them and how foremost to be happy and enjoy what life has to offer. The kids were touched and they wept openly. This was the essence of what was Sue. In her moment, when she could be feeling sorry for herself, she reached out to the boys and gave them the ability to move ahead, no matter what the future might hold for her. They have been given a blessing that everything would be all right and that life will go on. She gave them the chance to let go of their sadness and rejoice in what was ahead for them in their lives. How powerful is that? She had many high points in her life, but this had to be the summit—dying, yet still thinking of others.

Sue did the same with me. That evening she started to talk about plans. She wanted to die in our bed, no life support systems to be used. I couldn't bear to hear her talk this way, but she needed to. Sue was "cleaning" house, leaving things in fine order just to ease the pain and suffering for me and the kids. She told me not to dote on her, think about her and still love her, but not to get bogged down in sorrow. She continued by telling me that I was still a young man, I should go out, have fun the rest of my life, because Lord knows it hasn't been fun for me the past few years. Sue thanked me for all I had done for her and she told me that she was blessed that I was in her life. She said that she couldn't think of too many other men that would have stood by their wife's side as I did. I lost it on that one, crying out loud placing my head on her chest, howling as the tears were in free fall. With her only good arm, she stroked the back of my head, reassuring that everything was going to be all right. Almost as comic relief, Sue continued by suggesting that we needed a way to communicate after she was gone. We jokingly agreed that whenever the lights in the house flicker, that would be Sue's way of talking to me or watching over me. What a saint, giving, caring, loving to the very end.

This incredible woman, still thinking about me, went on to suggest something that she thought would comfort me later. Surprisingly, she told me that directly after she dies, everyone would be there for me, at the wake, the funeral, even a week later. But eventually these people would move on, whether it's to go back to work or tend to their own families and lives. They would leave, be out of the picture, and I'd be all alone. Seeing that I would need an emotional lift by then, she wanted me to throw a party and call it "Celebration For Susan," approximately thirty days after she died; a great big get-together with friends and family to reminisce about the good times, not the sadness of her loss. I told her that I would honor every request, but that it was not necessary just yet. There was still plenty more time to go. I just couldn't allow myself to succumb to the inevitable, especially in front of Sue.

I was receiving so many calls and e-mails asking about Sue's health, and all I could say was that it appeared that the end was near. You could hear the silence, the disbelief, the sadness, and the tears from Sue's friends, family, co-workers, and admirers. How could this woman, so full of life, so strong in will and body and heart, be at the end of this journey? There must be some mistake or something that could be done. These questions swirled in everyone's mind. They all wanted to help, but there was nothing that they could do at this time except pray, if they were religious, for Sue to be calm, peaceful, and pain free. Sue's physical needs were becoming greater and greater and more difficult for me to handle alone. She was like a limp paper doll that needed to be handled with special care. I had all I could do just to get her out of bed, into the wheelchair and onto a toilet seat when she had to go. It was now necessary to help feed her due to the fact that only one of her arms was mobile. Being never trained to care-give in this manner, it was time for me to seek help. I called the oncology nurses, our friends for over a decade. They were so sorry to hear all of this news about Sue's deteriorating condition and they hooked me up with a nurse, Rosie, who worked free-lance jobs and had much experience in end-of-life care at the patient's home. Rosie was a Godsend because she knew how to move Sue, how to hold her to prop her into correct positions, and knew how to show care that translated into respect and dignity for one's life.

Since Matthew went back to school, I was able to set up Rosie in his room. Matthew never had a television in his room, so I ran a cable on the floor into that room and took a television set from downstairs. Rosie was set up with all of the amenities she wanted. We also placed an old baby monitor receiver in the room so she could listen to Sue. By now Sue was sleeping for much of the time, getting weaker and frailer by the day, responding less and less to familiar voices. One of those shocking realizations hit me right between the eyes. Sue's body was shutting down to the point where she became incontinent. Rosie asked me to go to the grocery store and purchase adult diapers. This reminded me of the time at the start of all this when after her first few rounds of chemotherapy thirteen years ago Sue's hair was falling out in clumps. That was a traumatic reality check then as were the diapers now. It was hard to see these events occurring to your partner, your lover and best friend.

This was definitely taking its toll on me as well. Rosie cooked for Justin and me and tried desperately to force-feed us. I was losing weight at a rapid rate, probably close to fifty pounds due to my stress, anxiety, exhaustion and worry. I had no time to go to counseling at this point. My focus was here with Sue. Rosie strongly urged me to go out with some friends, have a few drinks, and escape for a while. Even though it was probably a good suggestion, I couldn't do it...not now...not after being side by side, step for step with Sue through it all.

We had made an appointment with the neurosurgeon a month before and tomorrow, Friday was the scheduled date. Sue was so out of it, sleeping, barely talking much at this point. I debated in my head whether or not I should keep this appointment. What would it do for Sue? Why do I want to disturb her from her peaceful surroundings at home to now dress her, get her into the wheelchair and somehow get her down the front steps, then drive into the city to appear in front of a doctor who probably wouldn't shed any new light on Sue's present condition anyway. I'll tell you why I did it—because I had promised Sue that I would leave no stone unturned until there was absolutely nothing remaining to try. This was probably my most foolish, selfish decision in this entire thirteen-year span. This visit was not going to miraculously bring Sue back but it would allow me to look in the mirror and say to myself, "I didn't let you down, Sue." In effect, keeping this scheduled appointment was not for Sue, it was for me!

I needed the aid of my burly neighbor to help Sue, slumped over in her wheelchair barely able to keep her head erect, amble and negotiate down my front steps. We got her into the car with Rosie's assistance and we drive off to the city, Sue, Rosie and I. We arrived after an hour on very congested roads, got Sue back into her chair, and went up the elevator to the second floor. First, she had blood taken, I'm not quite sure for what purpose, then we sat in the waiting room. All the while, Sue was hunched over occasionally awakening just to repose quickly again. It was now time to see the doctor. He saw Sue for the first time in a month and before he did any kind of examination on her, he spoke to me. His comment will forever stay etched in my mind. "My, her condition has really deteriorated in the past month. I had no idea." There was no need for anything further to be said or done. The three of us trekked back home and encountered the same difficulties we had before. Luckily, my neighbor was available once again to help us up the stairs and Rosie tucked Sue into bed. The trip was totally unnecessary. All it had accomplished was to agitate Sue from a restful, peaceful, serene setting at home, the place she really wanted to be all along. But I couldn't see the signs, or maybe more correctly, didn't want to.

After that ridiculous visit to the neurosurgeon, I came to terms with reality. The oncologist slammed me over the head with his "Joe" phone call, but that wasn't good enough for me. All the indicators were there, but I was blind. So that night, I threw down my weapons and surrendered to the obvious…cancer had won. Sue had already done this a month ago, but I refused until now. This was the most difficult night of my life, playing God, calling off the dogs, and admitting that it was now time to stop treatments, medicines, tests, scans and instead simply make Sue comfortable. No more poking, prodding, no more jaunts to see doctors. No, it was all over. An impossible phone call to have to make, I called a hospice service. A nice sounding person took down the information and said a nurse would be dropping by at the house tomorrow to begin proceedings. I broke down and cried as I shared the heart wrenching decision with Justin, explaining that hospice care will keep mom comfortable and pain free. He sobbed openly realizing that his mom's life was quickly ending. I hugged him and we cried together for a good long while. I called Matthew with the events of the day and told him my eventual determination that hospice care would be the best thing to do for mom at this time. He cried as well, and it hurt that I couldn't be there to hug him and comfort him in his time of sorrow. Rosie was there nodding her head knowing that this was the right thing to do for Sue. She had all too much experience with these kinds of situations. She came over to Justin and me and put her arms around us consoling us. She told us that Sue deserved to rest after her very long battle. It was definitely the correct course of action. She also shared other advice, which was powerful and really hit home with me. She suggested not remembering the last days only…try desperately recalling that a person is not just a moment in time but instead a glorious tapestry of a significant series of moments...an entire triumphant life resplendently marked by extraordinary elegance, beauty, and splendor. Rosie was so right. Her years of experience had shown through her very comforting words. I wrote an e-mail to everyone that Sue and I knew after talking to Rosie, Matthew and Justin and placing my hospice phone call:

Dear Friends and Family,

I know that all of you love Sue and care about her deeply. I have been overwhelmed but not surprised at the number of e-mails and phone calls that have come in. So many people love Sue. Forgive me for not getting in touch with each of you individually, but please be assured that I have done my best to tell Sue of your concerns for her. Please also know that it is not necessary for you to respond back to me, Sue and I know that you care, and at this time, my place is to be with her by her side.

This evening, we have instituted hospice care services at home, as per Sue's wishes. We have been informed by Sue's doctors that it is the appropriate thing to do at this time. I am very happy to tell you that she is not in any pain presently, and that is my main concern. I will try to keep you posted.

Thanks again for all the good wishes.

Joe

The next day, Saturday, I was more composed, almost as

if a weight had been lifted. I held it together when the hospice nurse arrived. We discussed what the hospice role would be making sure that Sue was comfortable. She mentioned a lot of people wait too long before using the services that hospice has to offer. I immediately hoped that was not the case with Sue, but I couldn't help thinking that my stubborn persistence to keep on trying put us in that category as well. But at this point, it didn't matter. I finally was doing right for Sue. She continued on to say that if necessary, morphine would be used to help if Sue experienced any pain. She walked on into the bedroom and with Sue sleeping restfully, didn't take her blood pressure or pulse. The nurse had a virtuous facial expression. I think she felt that appropriateness was being conducted here, and that seemed to be pleasing to her. She told me that she would be back tomorrow, but if needed for any reason at all I could call her on her cell phone.

All day long, I spent my time lying next to Sue in bed, sometimes stroking her forehead, her cheeks, her arms, and sometimes talking to her. She was no longer responding to any stimulus. Justin came into the room doing the same touching and conversing but Sue was no longer reacting. She just lay there in a seemingly peaceful supine position, expressionless, but still alive. Seeing her condition, I called Matthew at Berkeley and requested that he make the cross-country trip. He wasn't back at school for more than a week or two since the last visit, but Sue's very rapid health free-fall necessitated another plane trip home.

Later in the day, while I was lying down next to Sue

whispering into her ear, telling her how much I love her and that everything was going to be all right, the quiet of the room was suddenly interrupted by sounds and rustling from Sue. It appeared that she was beginning to have seizures. Her body jerked and convulsed, her mouth moved in kind of a chewing motion, and she began to sweat. I panicked and ran into Rosie's room. She hurried to Sue's side, stroking her and wiping off her brow with a towel. She verified that it did look as if Sue was seizing. The episode lasted an eternity but in reality probably ten minutes or so. When it was over, Sue's body reverted back to the same calmness she had demonstrated previously. Whether it was true or not, Rosie reassured me that Sue's actions were not causing her any pain or suffering. I resumed my vigilant watch over her not saying anything, just patiently watching. I even fell asleep for a while as the alluring environment in the room was a quiet darkness. I awoke after the catnap, and started to communicate with Sue once again, whispering my feelings for her. Thousands of thoughts were racing by me, thinking about the great life that we shared together. I talked to her about the fun things we did together asking her to remember this and remember that. At one point, I envisioned her getting up and responding to some of the queries I was asking. I talked to her about our beautiful kids, and how blessed I was to have had her in my life. Sue did respond, but not by talking. Instead she started seizing once again, her eyes fluttered, drool appeared by the corner of her mouth, her body shook with eerie twitching movements, and her heart was racing. While Rosie once again attended to Sue's radical symptoms, I walked out of the room and began to cry. I thought of two things regarding Sue's seizures. One was that they happened maybe coincidently maybe not, right after I spoke to her. Was this Sue's only method of communicating with me? Was this her attempt to respond to my words? I don't know for a fact, but no one to this day can tell me differently. She was trying so hard to acknowledge my presence in the room and even though she could no longer turn to me, hug me, and kiss me, she was doing just that in the only way her imprisoned body allowed her to. I could no longer stand to witness these violent motions. My second thought was more of a strong and urgent request. Seeing that I was not a religious person, I awkwardly looked towards the sky and screamed out, "Please take her now. I know Sue isn't coming back any longer. Please take her now." The rest of the evening was thank goodness, uneventful. The next morning rolled into early afternoon and no changes occurred. I was lying in my all too familiar position in bed next to Sue. She was laboring more than ever to get each intake of air. But even with that, she seemed at ease, her face was calm, and she seemed ready to move onward.

October 2, 2005. Does that date mean anything to you? Probably not. Sue, who touched down on this earth fifty-three years ago, after thirteen years of battle took her last breath at 2:35 p.m.

ABOUT THE AUTHOR

I must admit that I surprised myself in my ability to write this book. Mind you, I was a High School Math Teacher on Long Island by trade and taught for over thirty years on that level. Many of my closest "friends" suggested that I number or count the pages instead of attempting to write them, but I didn't let those "caustic" remarks deter me from my mission. My purpose in scripting this book was to aid people, educate them, and even lend them a chuckle or two.

I grew up in Brooklyn, NY under the Italian wings and watchful Catholic eyes of two wonderful parents, moved out on my own for a while, met the Jewish girl of my dreams, got married, and then started a family and new life out in the 'burbs on Long Island in Oceanside. I have lived a charmed life and am thankful for everything that it has to offer. *In Sickness and In Health: A Memoir of Love* allows you, the reader, to share in my, and my wife's experiences.

Hopefully the book will inspire you to constantly move forward in life, no matter how bad it may seem at times. Life is very precious. It is very fragile but it is the most beautiful thing we possess. Three lessons that Sue and I learned together in our journey are: 1) Absorb every moment, cherish the beauty that nature surrounds you with, a sunrise, a budding flower, a soaring bird, even an April rainfall. 2) Hold near and dear to your heart what you have, your friends and your family and 3) Most importantly, look to the future with love, hope and optimism…Sue and I accomplished it to the best of our ability…it's your turn now. Enjoy your exploration into the fullness of life!

Susan Satriano Foundation

♌♌♌

T his foundation is in honor of my wife, Susan. It is currently being funded from Sue's life insurance check, donations from friends, family and local businesses. That is where my book comes in. All net proceeds from the sale of this book will go to the Susan Satriano Memorial Scholarship Foundation which, as of this printing, has aided 33 high school students with $37,000. These monies are earmarked for their college education. To be eligible for the award they must be a graduating senior who plans to start college during the fall semester. They must have a parent who is deceased due to cancer, or have a parent who is presently battling it. The Foundation has been in existence for only 4 years and the number 33 is an astounding one. Mind you, many of these kids would never be eligible for academic awards simply because their grades suffer as they have to assume responsibilities that one or both parents can no longer handle. It is very important to keep the children of cancer parents, the "silent sufferers" in our daily stream of consciousness.

In Sickness and In Health
A Memoir of Love

For more information regarding J. S. Russo and his work,
visit his Web site: **www.SusanSatrianoFoundation.com**.

Additional copies of this book may be purchased online from
LegworkTeam.com; Amazon.com; BarnesandNoble.com;
Borders.com, or via the author's Web site:
www.SusanSatrianoFoundation.com.

You can also obtain a copy of the book by visiting L.I. Books
or ordering it from your favorite bookstore.

Breinigsville, PA USA
15 September 2009
224159BV00004B/17/P